Acrobat 8 Professional: Basic

Student Manual

ACE Edition

Acrobat 8 Professional: Basic

Series Product Managers:	Charles G. Blum and Adam A. Wilcox
Writer:	Dave Fink
Developmental Editor:	Brandon Heffernan
Copyeditor:	Cathy Albano
Keytester:	Cliff Coryea

Trademarks

ILT Series is a trademark of Axzo Press.

Some of the product names and company names used in this book have been used for identification purposes only and may be trademarks or registered trademarks of their respective manufacturers and sellers.

Disclaimers

We reserve the right to revise this publication and make changes from time to time in its content without notice.

The Adobe Approved Certification Courseware logo is either a registered trademark or trademark of Adobe Systems Incorporated in the United States and/or other countries. The Adobe Approved Certification Courseware logo is a proprietary trademark of Adobe. All rights reserved.

The ILT Series is independent from ProCert Labs, LLC and Adobe Systems Incorporated, and are not affiliated with ProCert Labs and Adobe in any manner. This publication may assist students to prepare for an Adobe Certified Expert exam, however, neither ProCert Labs nor Adobe warrant that use of this material will ensure success in connection with any exam.

Student Manual
ISBN-10: 1-4239-5495-5
ISBN-13: 978-1-4239-5495-8

Student Manual with data CD
ISBN-10: 1-4239-5497-1
ISBN-13: 978-1-4239-5497-2

Printed in the United States of America

1 2 3 4 5 6 7 8 9 10 GL 09 08 07

Contents

Introduction

After reading this introduction, you will know how to:

A Use ILT Series manuals in general.

B Use prerequisites, a target student description, course objectives, and a skills inventory to properly set your expectations for the course.

C Re-key this course after class.

Topic A: About the manual

ILT Series philosophy

Our manuals facilitate your learning by providing structured interaction with the software itself. While we provide text to explain difficult concepts, the hands-on activities are the focus of our courses. By paying close attention as your instructor leads you through these activities, you will learn the skills and concepts effectively.

We believe strongly in the instructor-led class. During class, focus on your instructor. Our manuals are designed and written to facilitate your interaction with your instructor, and not to call attention to manuals themselves.

We believe in the basic approach of setting expectations, delivering instruction, and providing summary and review afterwards. For this reason, lessons begin with objectives and end with summaries. We also provide overall course objectives and a course summary to provide both an introduction to and closure on the entire course.

Manual components

The manuals contain these major components:

- Table of contents
- Introduction
- Units
- Course summary
- Quick reference
- Glossary
- Index

Each element is described below.

Table of contents

The table of contents acts as a learning roadmap.

Introduction

The introduction contains information about our training philosophy and our manual components, features, and conventions. It contains target student, prerequisite, objective, and setup information for the specific course.

Units

Units are the largest structural component of the course content. A unit begins with a title page that lists objectives for each major subdivision, or topic, within the unit. Within each topic, conceptual and explanatory information alternates with hands-on activities. Units conclude with a summary comprising one paragraph for each topic, and an independent practice activity that gives you an opportunity to practice the skills you've learned.

The conceptual information takes the form of text paragraphs, exhibits, lists, and tables. The activities are structured in two columns, one telling you what to do, the other providing explanations, descriptions, and graphics.

Course summary

This section provides a text summary of the entire course. It is useful for providing closure at the end of the course. The course summary also indicates the next course in this series, if there is one, and lists additional resources you might find useful as you continue to learn about the software.

Quick reference

The quick reference is an at-a-glance job aid summarizing some of the more common features of the software.

Glossary

The glossary provides definitions for all of the key terms used in this course.

Index

The index at the end of this manual makes it easy for you to find information about a particular software component, feature, or concept.

Manual conventions

We've tried to keep the number of elements and the types of formatting to a minimum in the manuals. This aids in clarity and makes the manuals more classically elegant looking. But there are some conventions and icons you should know about.

Item	Description
Italic text	In conceptual text, indicates a new term or feature.
Bold text	In unit summaries, indicates a key term or concept. In an independent practice activity, indicates an explicit item that you select, choose, or type.
`Code font`	Indicates code or syntax.
`Longer strings of ▶ code will look ▶ like this.`	In the hands-on activities, any code that's too long to fit on a single line is divided into segments by one or more continuation characters (▶). This code should be entered as a continuous string of text.
Select **bold item**	In the left column of hands-on activities, bold sans-serif text indicates an explicit item that you select, choose, or type.
Keycaps like ↵ ENTER	Indicate a key on the keyboard you must press.

Hands-on activities

The hands-on activities are the most important parts of our manuals. They are divided into two primary columns. The "Here's how" column gives short instructions to you about what to do. The "Here's why" column provides explanations, graphics, and clarifications. Here's a sample:

Do it!

A-1:   Creating a commission formula

Here's how	Here's why
1 Open Sales	This is an oversimplified sales compensation worksheet. It shows sales totals, commissions, and incentives for five sales reps.
2 Observe the contents of cell F4	F4 ▼ = =E4*C_Rate The commission rate formulas use the name "C_Rate" instead of a value for the commission rate.

For these activities, we have provided a collection of data files designed to help you learn each skill in a real-world business context. As you work through the activities, you will modify and update these files. Of course, you might make a mistake and therefore want to re-key the activity starting from scratch. To make it easy to start over, you will rename each data file at the end of the first activity in which the file is modified. Our convention for renaming files is to add the word "My" to the beginning of the file name. In the above activity, for example, a file called "Sales" is being used for the first time. At the end of this activity, you would save the file as "My sales," thus leaving the "Sales" file unchanged. If you make a mistake, you can start over using the original "Sales" file.

In some activities, however, it might not be practical to rename the data file. If you want to retry one of these activities, ask your instructor for a fresh copy of the original data file.

Topic B: Setting your expectations

Properly setting your expectations is essential to your success. This topic will help you do that by providing:

- Prerequisites for this course
- A description of the target student
- A list of the objectives for the course
- A skills assessment for the course

Course prerequisites

Before taking this course, you should be familiar with personal computers and the use of a keyboard and a mouse. Furthermore, this course assumes that you've completed the following course or have equivalent experience:

- *Windows XP: Basic*

Target student

Students taking this course should be comfortable using a personal computer and Microsoft Windows XP. You should have little or no experience using Adobe Acrobat 8.0 Professional, but have probably viewed PDF files by using Adobe Reader or other PDF reader applications. You will get the most out of this course if your goal is to become proficient using Adobe Acrobat 8.0 Professional to create, modify, and review PDF documents.

Adobe ACE certification

This course is also designed to help you prepare for the Acrobat 8.0 ACE exam. For complete certification training, students should complete this course and *Acrobat 8.0 Professional: Advanced, ACE Edition.*

Course objectives

These overall course objectives will give you an idea about what to expect from the course. It is also possible that they will help you see that this course is not the right one for you. If you think you either lack the prerequisite knowledge or already know most of the subject matter to be covered, you should let your instructor know that you think you are misplaced in the class.

Note: In addition to the general objectives listed below, specific ACE exam objectives are listed at the beginning of each topic. For a complete mapping of ACE objectives to ILT Series content, see Appendix A.

After completing this course, you will know how to:

- Identify the benefits of PDF, navigate PDF documents by using bookmarks and links, search PDF documents, open and organize PDF documents by using the Organizer window, and access Acrobat help.

- Use the Adobe PDF printer to create a PDF document from any program's Print command, use the PDFMaker to create a PDF document from Microsoft applications, and use the Create PDF commands in Acrobat to create PDF documents from multiple files and from Web pages.

- Arrange pages within and between documents, modify PDF document text, add headers and footers, modify page numbering, move PDF document text and graphics to other programs, and apply password protection.

- Create bookmarks and modify bookmark destinations, arrange and nest bookmarks, format bookmarks, and create and format links.

- Enhance the accessibility of PDF documents and modify the Acrobat environment to suit needs or preferences.

- Secure PDF documents by applying passwords; digitally sign and validate digitally signed PDF files; encrypt PDF files based on user certificates; create a security envelope, encrypt PDF files by using Adobe Policy Server; and create password and certificate security policies.

- Prepare a PDF document for review, initiate automated reviews, use editing and markup tools to review a PDF document, organize and view comments from multiple reviewers, and create a comment summary PDF file.

Skills inventory

Use the following form to gauge your skill level entering the class. For each skill listed, rate your familiarity from 1 to 5, with 5 being the most familiar. *This is not a test.* Rather, it is intended to provide you with an idea of where you're starting from at the beginning of class. If you're wholly unfamiliar with all the skills, you might not be ready for the class. If you think you already understand all of the skills, you might need to move on to the next course in the series. In either case, you should let your instructor know as soon as possible.

Skill	1	2	3	4	5
Identifying the benefits of PDF					
Adjusting the magnification, view, and layout of a document					
Navigating PDF document pages					
Navigating a PDF document by using bookmarks and links					
Searching for specific text in a PDF document					
Finding text in a scanned document by using OCR					
Organizing PDF documents as a collection in the Organizer					
Finding help in using Acrobat					
Setting Acrobat application preferences					
Creating a PDF document from various sources, such as Microsoft Office applications, multiple files, and Web pages					
Arranging, extracting, and deleting PDF document pages					
Moving pages between PDF documents					
Editing and formatting PDF document text					
Adding headers and footers					
Modifying page numbering within Acrobat					
Copying text and graphics from a PDF document					
Adding, modifying, arranging, and formatting bookmarks					
Creating, resizing, and aligning links					
Creating links from selected text					
Optimizing PDF files					
Adding tags to a PDF file					
Checking the accessibility of a PDF file					

Skill	1	2	3	4	5
Fixing accessibility problems					
Modifying a tagged document's reading order					
Creating a new tag structure					
Using the Accessibility Setup Assistant					
Setting a Document Open password					
Setting a Permissions password					
Changing settings in a permissions-protected file					
Creating, exporting, and importing a digital ID					
Digitally signing a PDF document					
Validating a signed document					
Creating a blank digital signature field					
Certifying a PDF document					
Encrypting a PDF file by using a certificate					
Encrypting a PDF file by using Adobe Policy Server					
Creating a password security policy					
Applying a security policy					
Adding and opening an attachment					
Adding a background or watermark					
Initiating automated reviews					
Adding notes, text markups, and drawing markups					
Customizing the review author name					
Adding stamps					
Exporting and importing comments and markups					
Viewing, organizing, and summarizing comments from multiple reviewers					

Topic C: Re-keying the course

If you have the proper hardware and software, you can re-key this course after class. This section explains what you'll need in order to do so, and how to do it.

Hardware requirements

Your personal computer should have:

- A keyboard and a mouse
- An Intel Pentium III processor or equivalent
- 256 MB of RAM (512 MB recommended)
- 860 MB of available hard-disk space; cache for optional installation files (recommended) requires an additional 460 MB of available hard-disk space
- A CD-ROM drive for installation
- An XGA monitor at 1024×768 or higher resolution

Software requirements

You will also need the following software:

- Windows XP Professional, Windows XP Home Edition, or Windows 2000
- Adobe Acrobat 8.0 Professional
- Microsoft Word 2000 or later

Network requirements

The following network components and connectivity are also required for rekeying this course:

- Internet access, for the following purposes:
  - Downloading the latest critical updates and service packs from www.windowsupdate.com
  - Downloading the student data files from www.courseilt.com (if necessary)

Setup instructions to re-key the course

Before you re-key the course, you will need to perform the following steps.

1 Install Microsoft Windows XP on an NTFS partition according to the software manufacturer's instructions. If you have Internet access and are behind a software or hardware firewall, install the latest critical updates and service packs from www.windowsupdate.com. (You can also use Windows 2000, but the screen shots in this course were taken using Windows XP, so your screens might look somewhat different.)

2 Display file extensions.

    a Start Windows Explorer.

    b Choose Tools, Folder Options and select the View tab.

    c Clear the check box for Hide extensions for known file types and click OK.

    d Close Windows Explorer.

3   Install Adobe Acrobat 8.0 Professional according to the software manufacturer's instructions. Perform a typical installation. When prompted, accept the Acrobat license agreement, and then close Acrobat.

4   Install Microsoft Office 2000, XP, or 2003. Install only Microsoft Word. Only Word files are used in this course.

5   If necessary, reset any Acrobat defaults that you have changed. If you do not wish to reset the defaults, you can still re-key the course, but some activities might not work exactly as documented.

   a   Start Acrobat 8.0 Professional.

   b   Choose View, Toolbars, Reset Toolbars.

   c   Choose Advanced, Security Settings and in the Security Settings dialog box, select Digital IDs, select each digital ID (if any), and click Remove ID. Enter the necessary password and click OK (the passwords for this course were set to "password"). Close the Security Settings dialog box.

   d   Choose Edit, Preferences, and in the Preferences dialog box, select Commenting and check Always use Log-in Name for Author name.

   e   In the Preferences dialog box, select Identity and delete any text in the Name and Organization Name boxes.

   f   In the Preferences dialog box, select General and click Reset All Warnings. Click OK.

   g   Choose File, Organizer, Open Organizer to open the Organizer window. In the Categories pane, under Collections, click Progress report docs, press Delete, and click Yes to delete the collection. Close the Organizer window.

   h   Choose Advanced, Manage Trusted Identities to open the Manage Trusted Identities dialog box. In the Name list, select J Barclay (if present), click Delete, and click OK. Click Close.

   i   Close Acrobat 8.0 Professional.

6   Create a folder called Student Data at the root of the hard drive

7   Download the student data files for the course. You can download the data directly to your machine, or to a disk.

   a   Connect to www.courseilt.com/instructor_tools.html.

   b   Click the link for Adobe Acrobat to display a page of course listings, and then click the link for Acrobat 8.0 Professional: Basic, ACE Edition.

   c   Click the link for downloading the student data files and follow the instructions that appear on your screen.

CertBlaster exam preparation for ACE certification

CertBlaster pre- and post-assessment software is available for the Acrobat 8.0 ACE exam. To download and install this free software, complete the following steps:

1   Go to www.courseilt.com/certblaster.

2   Click the link for Acrobat 8.0.

3   Save the .EXE file to a folder on your hard drive. (Note: If you skip this step, the CertBlaster software will not install correctly.)

4   Click Start and choose Run.

5   Click Browse and then navigate to the folder that contains the .EXE file.

6   Select the .EXE file and click Open.

7   Click OK and follow the on-screen instructions. When prompted for the password, enter **c_acro8**.

Unit 1

Getting started

Unit time: 50 minutes

Complete this unit, and you'll know how to:

A Identify the benefits of PDF and the components of the Acrobat environment, and navigate in a PDF document.

B Use bookmarks and links to navigate a PDF document.

C Find specific text in a PDF document.

D Open recent documents and organize documents into collections.

E Get help using Acrobat.

F Specify Acrobat application preferences.

Topic A: The Acrobat environment

This topic covers the following ACE exam objectives for Acrobat 8.0 Professional.

#	Objective
1.2	Describe the options available for customizing toolbars.
2.1	Explain how to access and use navigation features in a PDF document.
2.3	Given a viewing tool, explain the purpose of or how to use that tool. (Tools include: Zoom, Scrolling, Go To, and Hand.)

PDF documents

Explanation

Acrobat 8.0 Professional allows you to convert documents from almost any program to the *Portable Document Format (PDF)*. Acrobat uses the Portable Document Format to preserve the fonts, layout, colors, and graphics of a document, regardless of the program or platform used to create the document. The result is a PDF file that looks the same as the original document. You typically can't open or edit the PDF document in the program in which it was originally created, often called the *source program* or authoring program.

The benefits of PDF

You can view a PDF document by using Acrobat, the free Adobe Reader, or another third-party PDF reader. PDF allows you to share documents with others who don't have the source program on their computers. Adobe Reader is available and free for both Windows and Macintosh.

PDF compresses content so that it can produce documents with significantly smaller file sizes than the original file. The smaller file sizes allow for more efficient sharing over e-mail and Internet transfers, because smaller files upload and download more quickly. You can also use Acrobat 8.0 to initiate a document review process, allowing multiple users to comment on and mark up PDF documents.

You can use Acrobat to secure a PDF document by restricting access to the file. You can specify passwords to control who can view, print, save, or modify a document. However, there are some limitations to what you can do with a document converted to PDF. While you can use Acrobat to perform certain editing functions, you don't have the same editorial control over a PDF document that you do over the original document created in the source program.

PDF files can store all the data needed to print a file to a desktop printer or a professional printer. PDF can embed all fonts and images within the file so that you can print the document without needing to reference external image or font files. Acrobat also provides *preflight* features that can help ensure a trouble-free printing process.

Do it!   **A-1: Identifying the benefits of PDF**

Questions and answers

1 How does PDF help you share documents with a diverse audience?

2 What is a benefit of using PDF for documents you distribute via the Internet?

3 How can you use Acrobat for collaborative projects?

4 How can you provide document security by using Acrobat?

5 What are some of the benefits of using PDF in a professional print production workflow?

The Getting Started window

Explanation

When you first start Adobe Acrobat 8.0, the Getting Started window opens, as shown in Exhibit 1-1. The Getting Started window provides quick links to help you get started using Acrobat, such as how to create PDF documents, combine and export documents, or work with forms. You can prevent the Getting Started window from appearing each time you start Acrobat by checking the "Do not show at startup" check box in the upper-right corner.

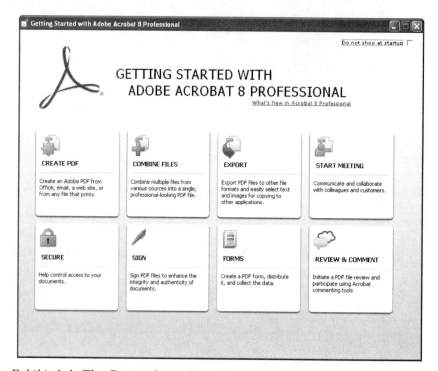

Exhibit 1-1: The Getting Started window

The Acrobat 8.0 interface

Some of the components in Acrobat 8.0 are activated only when you open a document. The default components of the Acrobat 8.0 interface are shown in Exhibit 1-2.

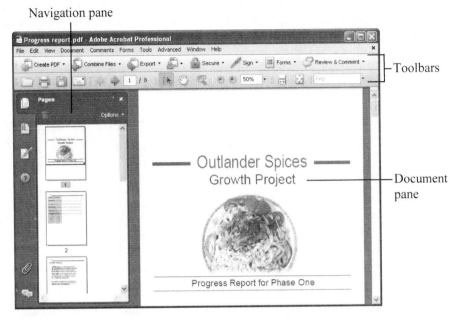

Exhibit 1-2: The default Acrobat 8.0 interface

The following table describes the major components of the Acrobat 8.0 interface.

Component	Description
Navigation pane	The navigation pane contains the Pages, Bookmarks, Signatures, How To, Attachments, and Comments icons. Activate these icons to navigate the document pages using bookmarks (if available) or page thumbnails, or to view signatures, attachments, or comments associated with the document.
Toolbars	By default, Acrobat 8.0 displays six toolbars that provide quick access to some of the most commonly used commands.
Document pane	The document pane displays the open document.

Toolbars

Several toolbars are open by default, and are docked to the top of the window. Although they appear as a single toolbar, "grabber bars" appear at the left edge of each toolbar, as shown in Exhibit 1-3. You can drag a grabber bar to reposition a toolbar or convert it to a floating toolbar. When you drag a toolbar away from the toolbar area, it becomes a floating toolbar that overlaps other Acrobat elements. To move a floating toolbar, drag it by its title bar. You can dock all the open toolbars by choosing View, Toolbars, Dock All Toolbars.

Grabber bars

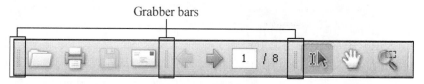

Exhibit 1-3: Grabber bars separate individual toolbars

To display or hide a particular toolbar, select View, Toolbars and then select the name of the toolbar that you want to display or hide. You can also display or hide a toolbar by right-clicking a blank area of the toolbar and selecting the name of the toolbar from the shortcut menu. To hide or display all the toolbars simultaneously, select View, Toolbars, Hide Toolbars, or press F8.

Most toolbars show only a basic set of default tools, but include other hidden tools. To view all the tools in a toolbar, right-click the toolbar grabber bar and choose Show All Tools. To reset the toolbar to the default tools, right-click the grabber bar and choose Reset Toolbar. Also, some toolbar buttons display their names next to the button icon. You can display or hide these button names by selecting an option from the View, Toolbars, Show Button Labels submenu.

To lock or unlock the positions of the toolbars in the toolbar area, select View, Toolbars, Lock Toolbars. When you lock the toolbars, the separator bars disappear, so you can no longer drag to reposition them. To display the default set of toolbars, choose View, Toolbars, Reset Toolbars.

The following table describes the default Acrobat 8.0 toolbars.

Toolbar	Description
Tasks	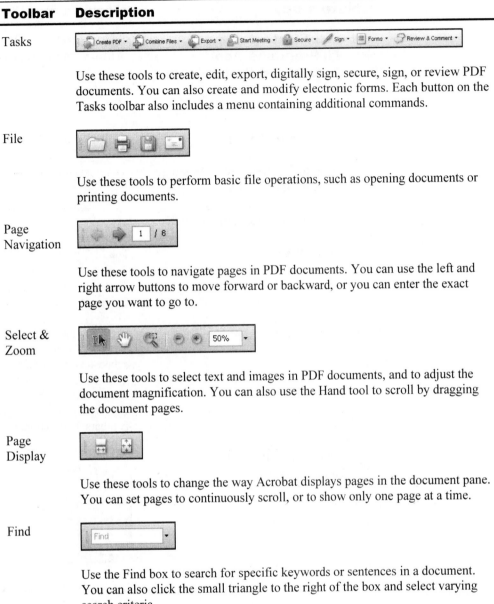 Use these tools to create, edit, export, digitally sign, secure, sign, or review PDF documents. You can also create and modify electronic forms. Each button on the Tasks toolbar also includes a menu containing additional commands.
File	Use these tools to perform basic file operations, such as opening documents or printing documents.
Page Navigation	Use these tools to navigate pages in PDF documents. You can use the left and right arrow buttons to move forward or backward, or you can enter the exact page you want to go to.
Select & Zoom	Use these tools to select text and images in PDF documents, and to adjust the document magnification. You can also use the Hand tool to scroll by dragging the document pages.
Page Display	Use these tools to change the way Acrobat displays pages in the document pane. You can set pages to continuously scroll, or to show only one page at a time.
Find	Use the Find box to search for specific keywords or sentences in a document. You can also click the small triangle to the right of the box and select varying search criteria.

Do it!

A-2:   Exploring the Acrobat environment

Here's how	Here's why
1 Click **Start** and choose **All Programs**, **Adobe Acrobat 8.0 Professional**	To start Acrobat 8.0. By default, the Getting Started window appears.
Close the Getting Started window	
2 Choose **File**, **Open...**	To display the Open dialog box.
From the Look in list, navigate to the current unit folder	
Select **Progress report.pdf**	
Click **Open**	The file opens in the document pane.
3 Locate the document pane	The document pane displays the current document.
4 Locate the menu bar	The menu bar is at the top of the Acrobat window. It contains menu items that allow you to take a variety of actions on a document.
5 Locate the toolbars	The toolbars are below the menu bar. You can hide or display the toolbars by selecting View, Toolbars, Hide Toolbars.
Point to the File toolbar grabber bar, as shown	
	To identify the toolbar. A tooltip appears with the toolbar's name.
Point to the Hand tool, as shown	
	A tooltip appears that describes what you can do with the Hand tool.

6   Point to the File toolbar grabber
    bar

    Drag the toolbar down into the   To make the File toolbar a floating toolbar.
    document pane   Changes you make to the work area remain in
                                        effect on your system until you further modify
                                        the work area.

    On the File toolbar, click the   To close the toolbar.
    Close button

7   Choose **View**, **Toolbars**, **File**   To open the File toolbar again. Notice that it's
                                        still a floating toolbar—Acrobat remembers
                                        your most recent setting. You'll return all
                                        toolbars to their default locations.

8   Choose **View**, **Toolbars**,   To reset the toolbars to their default location.
    Reset Toolbars

Views and navigation

Explanation   There are several ways to adjust your view of a document and navigate document pages. The technique you use will depend partly on your personal preferences and partly on the task at hand. For example, you'll use a different technique for navigating to the next page than you'd use for navigating 40 pages back in a large document.

The Select & Zoom toolbar

Zooming in and out is one way you can navigate within document pages. You can adjust document magnification by using tools in the Select & Zoom toolbar. By default, only some of the tools are visible, but you can view all the tools by right-clicking the toolbar grabber bar and choosing Show All Tools. The expanded toolbar is shown in Exhibit 1-4. You can also access most of these tools by using the appropriate commands in the View menu.

Select & Zoom toolbar

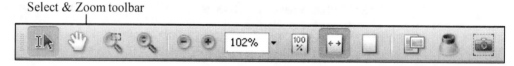

Exhibit 1-4: The expanded Select & Zoom toolbar

The following table describes some commonly used zoom tools.

Tool	Description
	You can use the Marquee Zoom tool in several ways. Drag to create a rectangle around an area so that it fills the viewing area, or click the document to increase magnification. You can also Ctrl-click to decrease magnification. Each click increases/decreases magnification one preset level.
	You can use the Dynamic Zoom tool to zoom in and out by dragging up and down on the document. Dragging up increases magnification and dragging down decreases magnification.
102%	Use the Zoom menu to select a specific magnification percentage. You can also type a percentage in the box and press Enter.
	Click the Zoom In/Out buttons to increase/decrease the document magnification without having to select a zoom tool. You can continue working with whatever tool you already had selected.
100%	Click the Actual Size button to display a document at its actual size, or 100%. Depending on the size of your monitor and the size of the viewing area, the full area of the page might not be visible at 100%.
	Click the Fit Page button to display the entire page. The resulting magnification level will vary depending on the size of your monitor and the size of the viewing area.
←→	Click the Fit Width button to view a document's entire width in the document pane. You won't have to scroll horizontally to view any area of a page. The resulting magnification level will vary depending on the size of your monitor and the size of the viewing area.

Zoom shortcuts

You can also use keyboard shortcuts to select zoom commands and to access zoom tools. The following table describes several zooming shortcuts.

Shortcut	Description
Ctrl+Spacebar	Temporarily selects the Marquee Zoom tool for increasing magnification. Releasing Ctrl+Spacebar returns you to the tool you were using previously.
Ctrl+Spacebar+Alt	Temporarily selects the Marquee Zoom tool for decreasing magnification. You have to press Ctrl+Spacebar and then also hold Alt to make the switch.
Ctrl+0	Zooms to Fit Page magnification.
Ctrl+1	Zooms to Actual Size magnification.
Ctrl+2	Zooms to Fit Width magnification.

The Page Navigation toolbar

The Page Navigation toolbar contains buttons you can use to navigate between document pages. Again, only some of the tools are visible in the toolbar by default, but you can expand it by right-clicking the toolbar grabber bar and choosing Show All Tools.

Page Navigation toolbar

Exhibit 1-5: The expanded Page Navigation toolbar

The following table describes the buttons on the Page Navigation toolbar.

Tool	Description
	Click the First/Last Page buttons to navigate to the first page or last page of the document.
	Click the Next/Previous Page buttons to navigate backward or forward one page in the document.
	Enter a page number in the box to navigate directly to that page. The Page Number box displays the number of the page you're viewing and the total number of pages in the document.
	Click the Previous/Next View buttons to navigate to the view you were using previously. A view is specific content shown at a specific magnification. (For example, viewing a particular block of text or image on page 3 at 120% magnification.) If you navigate directly from page 7 to page 18 using the Current page box, for example, you could click the Previous View button to return to page 7.

The navigation pane

You can also navigate between document pages by using the navigation pane. The navigation pane contains icons you can click to view document page thumbnails, bookmarks, signatures, or comments. There are several techniques you can use when working with the navigation pane.

- In the navigation pane, click an icon to show or hide the associated panel.
- Choose a navigation panel from the View, Navigation panels submenu to show or hide that panel.
- Press F4 to open or close the navigation pane.

The View, Navigation Panels submenu also includes panels that aren't included in the navigation pane by default. If a panel is not included, you can select it from the submenu to open it as a floating panel, and then drag the floating panel to the navigation pane to store it there. You can also drag any panel away from the navigation pane to remove it. To reset the navigation pane to display the default panels, choose View, Navigation Panels, Reset Panels. Finally, you can adjust the width of the navigation pane by dragging its right edge.

The Pages panel

You also can use the Pages panel to navigate document pages. To view the Pages panel, click the Pages icon in the navigation pane. When you do, the panel shows thumbnails of all the pages in the document that you can click to go to different pages. If the document pages are too large to display completely in the document pane, a red border appears on the thumbnail to represent the area visible in the document pane. You can drag the red border to scroll the content in the document pane. To drag the red border, point to its edge, as shown in Exhibit 1-6, and then drag.

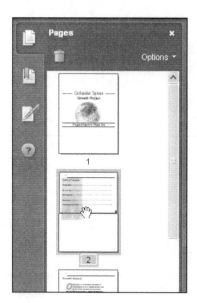

Exhibit 1-6: The Pages panel

The Page Display toolbar

You can use the tools in the Page Display toolbar to change the way pages are displayed in the document pane. Exhibit 1-7 shows the expanded toolbar.

Page Display toolbar

Exhibit 1-7: The expanded Page Display toolbar

There are four page layout views that you can apply. The following table describes these page layout options.

Button	Example	Description
		The Single Page button displays one page at a time in the document pane.
		The Single Page Continuous button displays pages in a continuous vertical column. You can scroll to display more than one page at a time.
		The Two-Up button displays pages in a spread side by side. You can view only one spread at a time.
		The Two-Up Continuous button displays pages side by side in a continuous vertical column.

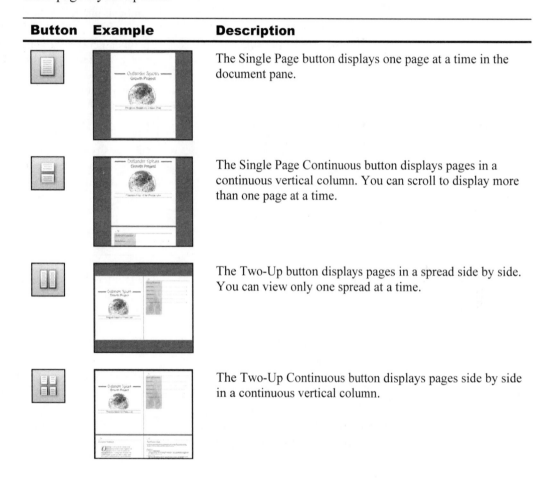

A-3: Viewing and navigating a PDF document

Here's how	Here's why
1 In the navigation pane, click the Pages icon	
	To display the Pages panel. You can now see thumbnail images of the document pages.
2 Click the top of the Page 4 thumbnail	The document pane displays the top portion of Page 4. The red border on the page thumbnail represents the part of the document displayed in the document pane.
Point to the edge of the Page 4 thumbnail's red border	
	The pointer changes to a hand, indicating that you can drag the red border to scroll through the document.
Drag the red border downward	To scroll down the page in the document pane.
Drag the red border to the thumbnail's top-left corner	To display the top-left corner of the page in the document pane.
3 Right-click the Select & Zoom toolbar's grabber bar, as shown	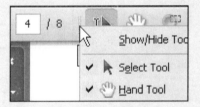
	To display a toolbar drop-down list.
Choose **Show All Tools**	To show all the hidden tools in the toolbar.

4 On the expanded toolbar, click	(The Fit Width button.) The page's width fits to the width of the document pane.
5 On the toolbar, click	To select the Marquee Zoom tool.
Click once anywhere on the page	To zoom in one preset level.
6 Press and hold (CTRL)	When you do, the plus sign on the tool changes to a minus sign.
Click anywhere on the page	To zoom out one preset level.
7 On the toolbar, click	To select the Select tool.
Point anywhere on the page	
8 Press and hold (CTRL) + (SPACEBAR)	To temporarily select the Marquee Zoom tool without clicking it in the toolbar. If you click using this key combination, you'll zoom in one preset level.
Drag as shown	
	To select an area to zoom in on.
Release the mouse button	To zoom in on the area.
9 Press and hold (CTRL) + (SPACEBAR) + (ALT)	The plus sign on the tool changes to a minus sign. If you click using this key combination, you'll zoom out one preset level.
Release the keys	To return to the Select tool.
10 On the toolbar, click	(The Fit Page button.) To fit the entire page in the document pane.

11	Right-click the Page Display toolbar's grabber bar, as shown	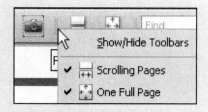
		To display a toolbar drop-down list.
	Choose **Show All Tools**	To show all the hidden tools in the toolbar. (The toolbar drops down a level to show all the tools.)
12	On the expanded toolbar, click	(The Single Page Continuous button.) With this option selected, you can scroll through the pages.
13	On the Select & Zoom toolbar, click	(The Hand tool.) You'll use this tool to navigate in the document.
	Point near the middle of the page, and drag upward	To begin scrolling to the next page.
14	On the Page Display toolbar, click	The Single Page button.
	Point near the middle of the page, and drag upward	In single page view, you cannot use the Hand tool to scroll between pages. To move to other pages, you need to click in the vertical scroll bar, or click a thumbnail in the navigation pane.
15	In the navigation pane, scroll up to the beginning of the document	If necessary.
	Click the Page 1 thumbnail	To jump to the first page of the document.

Topic B: Advanced navigation

This topic covers the following ACE exam objective for Acrobat 8.0 Professional.

#	Objective
2.1	Explain how to access and use navigation features in a PDF document.

Bookmarks and links

Explanation

In addition to Acrobat's standard options for navigating pages, some PDF documents include bookmarks and links that you can use to navigate directly to specific content.

The Bookmarks panel

To view a document's bookmarks, open the Bookmarks panel, shown in Exhibit 1-8, by clicking the Bookmarks icon in the navigation pane. Some applications automatically generate bookmarks when converting documents to PDF, but you can also modify or add bookmarks within Acrobat. Bookmarks are often set up as a sort of table of contents.

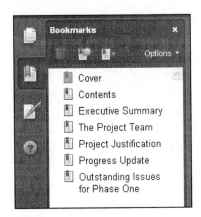

Exhibit 1-8: The Bookmarks panel

Do it!

B-1: Navigating with bookmarks

Here's how	Here's why
1 In the navigation pane, click the Bookmarks icon	
	To open the Bookmarks panel in the navigation pane.
2 Observe the current magnification	The document magnification is set to Fit Page, so that an entire page fits in the document pane.
3 Click the bookmark labeled **Project Justification**	To navigate to the bookmark's location. The bookmark navigates to page 6 and changes the magnification to Fit Width.
4 Explore the other bookmarks	

Links

Links in Acrobat 8.0 work similarly to links on Web pages. A link in Acrobat allows you to jump to another section in a document. For example, you can link a table of contents entry to its corresponding content in the document. Links can also navigate to specific sections within another PDF document. They can even open another document. For example, a link to a Word document can open that document in Word. Links can also point to Internet addresses.

Do it!

B-2: Navigating with links

Here's how	Here's why
1 In the Bookmarks panel, click **Contents**	The table of contents in this document contains links to each section.
2 On the Table of Contents page, point to the section names	*Table of Contents* *Executive Summary*............................ The pointer changes to a pointing finger when it passes over a link.
3 Click **Project Justification**	The document pane displays Page 6.
4 In the Bookmarks panel, click **Contents**	To return to the table of contents.
5 Explore the other links	(Click them.) To navigate to other linked sections of the document.

Topic C: Finding text

This topic covers the following ACE exam objective for Acrobat 8.0 Professional.

#	Objective
2.2	Use Find/Search to locate specific information in PDF documents.

Find and Search

Explanation

There are several techniques you can use to search for specific text in a PDF document. The two primary search methods are *Find* and *Search*. Each provides options that are appropriate to different situations.

The Find toolbar

The simplest way to search a PDF document is to type the text you want to look for in the Find toolbar. When you start a search, the Find Previous and Find Next buttons appear. Clicking these buttons takes you to the previous or next occurrence of the text.

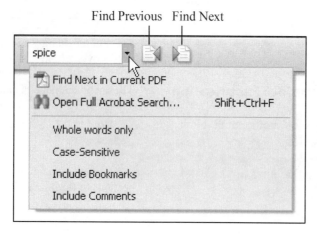

Exhibit 1-9: The Find toolbar with the Find Options list visible

The Find Options list provides several search options that you can choose from, as shown in Exhibit 1-9. The following table describes some of these options.

Option	Description
Whole words only	Search for an exact word or phrase in the document. Only exact matches will appear in the search results. Conversely, clearing this option will find any word containing the search term. For example, searching for "live" would return "live," "lives," and "enliven."
Case-Sensitive	Search for words whose capitalization matches that of the search term you specify.
Include Bookmarks	Search within bookmark titles as well as the rest of the document. If the Bookmarks tab is not active, clicking the search result located in a bookmark will activate it.
Include Comments	Search comments from those who have reviewed the document.

Do it!   ## C-1: Finding text by using the Find toolbar

Here's how	Here's why
1 In the Bookmarks panel, click **Cover**	To jump to the first page of the document.
2 In the Find toolbar, type **spice**	spice│ ▾
Press (↵ ENTER)	The word is highlighted on the page. Also, the Find Previous and Find Next buttons appear.
3 Click the Find Next button	To go to the next occurrence of the word.
4 Click the Find Next button several more times	To find each instance of the word throughout the document. Clicking the Find Previous button will cycle backward through the search results.

The Search window

Explanation

You can also search documents by using the Search window, shown in Exhibit 1-10. To open the Search window, select Open Full Acrobat Search from the Find Options list in the Find toolbar or choose Edit, Search.

Exhibit 1-10: The Search window

To locate terms by using the Search window:

1   In the box at the top of the Search window, enter the word or phrase you want to locate.

2   Specify the location in which you want to search.

- To search only the current file, select In the current PDF document.

- To search all files stored in a given location, select All PDF Documents in; then select the location from the drop-down list.

3   Specify any additional options you want to use to restrict the search results.

4   Click Search. The search results appear in the Search window.

5   In the Results list, click an item to view that instance of the word on the document page where it's located.

6   To perform another search, click New Search in the Search window.

Do it!

C-2: Finding text by using the Search PDF window

Here's how	Here's why
1 From the Find Options list, select **Open Full Acrobat Search...**	(In the Find toolbar.) To open the Search window. You'll search for the word "product."
2 Type **product**	(In the What word or phrase would you like to search for? Box.) You'll search the document for all instances of the word.
Click **Search**	The Search window displays a list of results, with the search term highlighted. The search results include the words product, products, and productivity.
Click the third item in the Results list	To view that item in the document. The document pane displays Page 6.
3 Observe the highlighted text in the document	The specific occurrence of the search term is highlighted in the document pane.
4 Click other items in the Results list	To view the other occurrences of the search term.
5 In the Search window, click **New Search**	To search for a new term. The previous search term appears in the search text box.
6 Edit the search text to read **project**	
Check **Whole words only**	To locate only instances of the exact word.
Click **Search**	
Observe the search results	Only whole forms of the word are listed. For example, the results don't include terms such as projects, projected, or projections. However, because you didn't check Case-Sensitive, you find both capitalized and lowercase instances of the word.
7 Close the Search window	
8 Close the document	If a dialog box appears asking if you want to save your changes, click No.

Optical character recognition (OCR)

Explanation

Scanned documents are typically saved in image formats, which means that any text contained within them cannot be searched. Acrobat 8.0 can apply *optical character recognition (OCR)* to make the text searchable. It works on any scanned document that contains clean, legible text. Applying OCR to a document will not make the text editable. Searchable documents contain the original image files of scanned documents in the foreground and searchable text in an invisible background layer. OCR will work with images that have been scanned at 144 ppi or higher. In general, the higher the resolution, the better the character recognition.

To apply OCR to a scanned document:

1 Open the scanned document in Acrobat.

2 Choose Document, OCR Text Recognition, Recognize Text Using OCR.

3 In the Recognize Text dialog box, choose whether to apply OCR to the current page only, to all pages in the document, or to a range of pages.

4 Under Settings, click the Edit button to open the Recognize Text - Settings dialog box.

5 Change the Primary OCR Language, if necessary.

6 Choose Searchable Image (Exact) to create an invisible layer of searchable text behind the original scanned image. Choose Searchable Image (Compact) to compress the foreground image, reducing file size but also reducing image quality. Choose Formatted Text & Graphics to reproduce the original page using recognized fonts, graphics, and other elements.

7 Click OK.

Do it!

C-3: Finding text by using OCR

Here's how	Here's why
1 Open Scanned document.pdf	(From the current unit folder.) This document was scanned as an image and converted to PDF.
2 Using the Find toolbar, search for the word "project"	(In the Find toolbar, enter "project" and press Enter.) A window appears and indicates that the item was not found.
Click **OK**	
3 Choose **Document, OCR Text Recognition, Recognize Text Using OCR...**	To open the Recognize Text dialog box.
Click **OK**	To apply OCR to the document.
4 Use the Find toolbar to search for the word "project"	This time, the search term is highlighted in the document.
5 Save the document as **OCR document**	In the current unit folder.
6 Close the document	

Topic D: Organizing PDF documents

The Organizer

Explanation

You can access recent PDF documents by using Acrobat's Organizer. You can also use the Organizer to group PDF documents for easy retrieval. The *Organizer,* shown in Exhibit 1-11, helps you browse a list of recent PDF documents you have viewed and organize your documents into collections.

Collections

Collections are groups of PDF documents that you've associated with a particular folder in the Organizer. Collection folders contain aliases of PDF documents, so you can associate any PDF document with any collection without changing the location of the document on your computer. The Organizer shows previews of recently viewed PDF documents (up to the last 12 months). You can also use the Organizer to browse PDF files and perform actions on PDF documents.

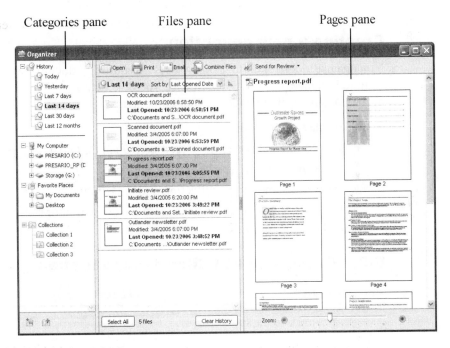

Exhibit 1-11: The Organizer

The Categories pane is divided into three sections: History, My Computer and Favorite Places, and Collections. The History section groups PDF documents opened in the last 12 months and displays them in the Files pane. The Pages pane shows a preview of the document pages. In the Categories pane, use My Computer to browse for PDF documents on your computer and Favorite Places to find commonly used folders. The Collections section contains folders that list the PDF files you've associated with a particular collection.

To open the Organizer, expand the Files toolbar, and then click the Organizer button. Or, you can choose File, Organizer, Open Organizer.

Do it!

D-1: Browsing recent PDF documents

Here's how	Here's why
1 Choose **File, Organizer, Open Organizer**	To open the Organizer window.
2 Locate the History pane	Documents from the last 12 months are grouped into folders.
In the History pane, click **Today**	To view documents you've opened today.
3 Locate the Files pane	Recently viewed documents are displayed here.
In the Files pane, click **Progress report**	The Pages pane displays a navigable preview of the document.
In the Files pane, double-click **Progress report**	To open the document.

Creating a new collection

Explanation

You can use a collection to group aliases of your PDF documents. This way, when you want to organize your PDF documents, you don't have to change the physical location of the documents that reside on your computer.

To make a new collection:

1 If necessary, choose File, Organizer, Open Organizer to open the Organizer.
2 Click the Create a new collection button.
3 Enter the name of the collection and press Enter.
4 Drag items from the Files pane into the collection or right-click the collection and choose Add Files.

Do it!

D-2: Organizing PDF files as a collection

Here's how	Here's why
1 Switch back to the Organizer	
2 Click the **Collection 1** folder, as shown	
	(In the Categories pane.) To view the documents in this collection. This sample folder is empty. Acrobat displays help text about collections.

3	In the bottom-left corner of the Organizer, click 🔲	(The Create a new collection button.) You'll create a new collection.
	Enter **Progress Report docs**	To name the collection.
4	In the History pane, click **Today**	To view recent documents.
5	In the Files pane, click the Progress report icon	To select it.
	Press and hold (CTRL)	
	Click OCR document	To select the two documents at once. You'll add aliases for these documents to the collection.
	Release (CTRL)	
6	Drag the icons to the Progress Report docs folder, as shown	
7	Click the Progress Report docs collection	To verify that the documents are in the collection.
8	Right-click the Progress Report docs collection	A shortcut menu appears.
	Choose **Add Files...**	To display the Select files to add to your collection dialog box.
9	Select Add to collection.pdf	In the current unit folder.
	Click **Add**	To add an alias of this document to the collection.
10	Close the Organizer	

Topic E: Getting help

Getting help

Explanation

Acrobat 8 provides several ways to get help performing tasks in your documents. You can get help using the Tasks toolbar or the How To panel, and by opening the Help system.

The Tasks toolbar

The Tasks toolbar is visible by default at the top of the application window. Each of the buttons on the toolbar corresponds to common tasks, such as creating PDF files, combining or exporting files, or working with forms. Each button also includes a drop-down list with additional commands. At the bottom of each list is a "Getting Started with" command. When you select the command, the Getting Started window opens and provides information about the task you selected, as shown in the example in Exhibit 1-12. You can click links in the window to begin performing tasks, or to navigate to more information.

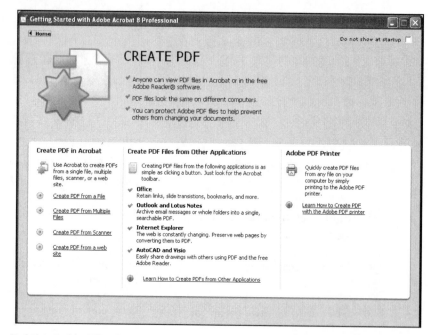

Exhibit 1-12: The Getting Started window for the Create PDF task

The How To panel

You can also access common help topics by clicking the How To button in the navigation pane, which opens the How To panel, shown in Exhibit 1-13. Similar to the Tasks toolbar, the How To panel provides links to assist you with common tasks. However, instead of opening the Quick Start window, clicking the links simply provides help information within the panel.

Exhibit 1-13: The How To panel

The Help Viewer

You can also search for information by choosing Help, Complete Adobe Acrobat 8.0 Professional Help, or by clicking the Complete Acrobat 8.0 Help link in the How To panel. When you do, the Adobe Help Viewer opens in a separate window, as shown in Exhibit 1-14. From here, you can look for help information by using the Contents, Index, and Search tabs. Each link you click in the navigation pane displays corresponding information in the topic pane.

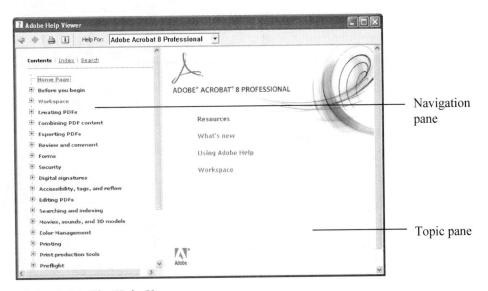

Exhibit 1-14: The Help Viewer

Do it!

E-1: Finding information

Here's how	Here's why
1 Click the Create PDF button	
	(In the Tasks toolbar.) To view the button list.
Select **Getting Started with Create PDF**	The Getting Started window opens and displays information and links about creating PDFs.
Close the Getting Started window	
2 In the navigation pane, click	(The How To button.) To open the How To panel.
Click **Acrobat Essentials**	The How To window changes to show help topics for common Acrobat tasks.
At the top of the panel, click	(The Home Page button.) To return to the How To panel home page.
3 Click **Complete Acrobat 8.0 Help**	(At the bottom of the How To panel.) To open the Help Viewer.
Maximize the window	If necessary.
4 Click **Search**	You'll enter a help topic.
5 Type **commenting**	
	To search for information on commenting in a PDF document.
Click **Search**	
6 Explore the search results	(Click the topics.) The help information for the selected topic appears in the topic pane.
7 Close the Help Viewer	
8 Close the document	

Topic F: Preferences

Setting Acrobat preferences

Explanation

Acrobat uses certain default settings that affect how the application functions and displays PDF documents. You can use the Preferences dialog box to customize many of these settings to suit your workflow.

The Preferences dialog box

The settings you specify in the Preferences dialog box control how Acrobat functions. Although many of these settings affect how PDF documents appear and function on your system, they won't affect how those same PDF documents appear in Acrobat on another user's system.

To specify Acrobat application preferences:

1   Choose Edit, Preferences to open the Preferences dialog box.
2   On the left side of the dialog box, select a category to display its options.
3   Specify the settings you want to use for the selected preference category.
4   Click OK.

Do it!

F-1:   Setting Acrobat application preferences

Here's how	Here's why
1 Choose **Edit**, **Preferences...**	To open the Preferences dialog box.
2 In the Categories list, click **Documents**	To view document preferences. By default, the bottom portion of the File menu lists the five most recently opened files. You'll change this setting so that it shows only the three most recently opened files.
3 Under Open Settings, in the Documents in recently used list box, enter **3**	
4 Click **OK**	As you open files from this point forward, Acrobat will remember the three most recent files and list them in the File menu so you can access them quickly.

Unit summary: Getting started

Topic A   In this topic, you learned about the benefits of **PDF**. You identified components of the **Acrobat 8.0 interface**, and you learned how to **navigate** a PDF document and modify viewing options.

Topic B   In this topic, you learned how to use existing **bookmarks** and **links** to navigate a PDF document.

Topic C   In this topic, you learned how to find text in a PDF document by using the **Search PDF window** and the **Find toolbar**. You also learned how to search text in a scanned document by using **OCR**.

Topic D   In this topic, you learned how to use the **Organizer** to view your recently opened PDF documents and how to group PDF documents into **collections**.

Topic E   In this topic, you learned how to use Acrobat's **Help** and **How To** features to find information about using Acrobat.

Topic F   In this topic, you learned how to use the Preferences dialog box to specify Acrobat **application preferences**.

Independent practice activity

In this activity, you'll open a PDF document and navigate it using several different methods. You'll also search for specific text in the document, and use OCR to search through scanned text.

1 From the current unit folder, open Outlander newsletter.pdf. Save the document as **My Outlander newsletter** in the current unit folder.

2 Change the layout view to Continuous. (*Hint:* In the Page Display toolbar, click the Single Page Continuous button.)

3 Use the Hand Tool to navigate to page 2. (*Hint:* Using the Hand tool, drag up to scroll to the next page.)

4 Temporarily select the Marquee Zoom tool and zoom in on the About Us paragraph. (*Hint:* Press and hold Ctrl+Spacebar to temporarily select the Marquee Zoom tool; then click (or drag) the About Us paragraph to zoom in on it.)

5 Change the magnification to 200%. (*Hint*: Use the Select & Zoom toolbar's Magnification box to enter or select the magnification value.)

6 View bookmarks and navigate to the Contents section. (*Hint*: In the navigation pane, click the Bookmarks icon; then click the Contents bookmark.)

7 In the table of contents, use the links to go to the Spice Tips section.

8 Search for **incentive plan**. (*Hint*: Use Find or Search. The search term isn't found because the text in the document is not searchable.)

9 View page 7 at Fit Width magnification. (*Hint:* To navigate to page 7, click the Pages icon in the navigation pane, and then click the Page 7 icon.)

10 Apply OCR to page 7. (*Hint*: Choose **Document, OCR Text Recognition, Recognize Text Using OCR** to open the Recognize Text dialog box. Select **From page**, and enter **7** for both values.)

11 Search for **incentive plan** again.

12 Save and close the document.

Review questions

1 Which statements are true about showing and hiding toolbars? (Choose all that apply.)

  A You can display or hide a toolbar by right-clicking the toolbar area and selecting the name of the toolbar from the shortcut menu.

  B You can convert a docked toolbar to a floating toolbar by dragging its grabber bar away from the toolbar area.

  C You can hide all toolbars by choosing View, Toolbars, Hide Toolbars.

  D You can hide or display all toolbars by pressing Tab.

2 Which key combination temporarily selects the Zoom tool and lets you zoom out?

  A Ctrl+Spacebar

  B Ctrl+Spacebar+Alt

  C Ctrl+Shift+Alt

  D Ctrl+Shift

3 Which tool can you use to scroll from one page to the next by dragging?

  A The Loupe tool

  B The Hand tool

  C The Zoom In tool

  D The Select tool

4 Which are valid ways to navigate a document? (Choose all that apply.)

  A Open the Bookmarks panel and click a bookmark to jump to a specific page.

  B Within a page, click a link.

  C Right-click a page in the document; then choose a new page from the page list.

  D Use the Hand tool to drag from one page to another.

5 Which statements about the Pages panel are true? (Choose all that apply.)

  A To view the Pages panel, click the Pages icon in the navigation pane.

  B If the document pages are too large to appear completely in the document pane, a red border appears on the thumbnail to represent the visible area.

  C To navigate to a different page in the document, click one of the page thumbnails.

  D To add a new page to a document, double-click one of the pages thumbnails.

6 You want to locate all instances of a particular word in a document. What's the simplest way to search for the word?

   A Enter the word in the Find toolbar and press Enter.

   B Select an instance of the word in the document and press Ctrl+F.

   C Choose Edit, Search, enter the word you are looking for, and press Enter.

   D Select an instance of the word in the document and choose Edit, Find.

7 How can you open the Search window? (Choose all that apply.)

   A Choose Edit, Search.

   B Press Ctrl+S.

   C In the Find toolbar, from the Find Options drop-down list, select Open Full Acrobat Search.

   D Double-click the text box in the Find toolbar.

8 Which command should you use to view information about PDF files you've opened recently on your computer?

   A Edit, Find

   B File, Organizer, Open Organizer

   C Edit, Search

   D View, Navigation Tabs, Destinations

9 How can you view common help topics while still viewing the current document in Acrobat?

   A Choose Help, Complete Adobe Acrobat 8.0 Professional Help.

   B Choose Help, About Adobe Acrobat 8.0 Professional.

   C Choose from the Help, How To submenu.

   D In the How To window, click Complete Adobe Acrobat 8.0 Professional Help.

10 Which statement is true about settings you specify by choosing Edit, Preferences?

   A They affect the current document only.

   B They affect documents you've already created, but not new documents you create.

   C They affect how documents you create function on other people's systems.

   D They affect how Acrobat functions on your system.

Unit 2

Converting documents to PDF

Unit time: 45 minutes

Complete this unit, and you'll know how to:

A Create a PDF document from any program's Print command.

B Create PDF documents from Microsoft applications by using PDFMaker.

C Create PDF documents from multiple files and from Web pages.

Topic A: Printing to PDF from any application

This topic covers the following ACE exam objective for Acrobat 8.0 Professional.

#	Objective
3.2	Create a PDF document by using Adobe PDF Printer.

Creating a PDF document

Explanation

There are several ways that you can create a PDF document from an existing document. When you create a PDF document, the original document is not replaced by the PDF version. If you have Acrobat installed, you'll see that many of your applications include commands that allow you to convert files to PDF directly from that application, without having to open Acrobat. There are several techniques you can use to create a PDF document:

- Use PDFMaker (available in some applications)
- Use the Adobe PDF printer (from any application with a Print command)
- Use the Create PDF menu (within Acrobat)

The Abobe PDF printer

The *Adobe PDF printer* can convert a file created in any application to a PDF document. When you install Acrobat 8.0, the Adobe PDF printer is automatically added to the list of available printers. The Adobe PDF printer converts a file to PostScript format, and then sends the PostScript file to Distiller, which converts the PostScript file to PDF. *Distiller* converts PostScript files to PDF automatically, and is included in the Acrobat installation. You can launch Distiller directly, and use it to convert a PostScript file to PDF. However, because Distiller converts only PostScript files, it's more convenient to use the PDF printer, which converts any file type to PostScript for you, and sends it to Distiller for conversion to PDF.

To create a PDF document by using the Adobe PDF printer:

1. Open the file in its source application (for example, Microsoft Word or WordPad).
2. Choose File, Print. The Print dialog box appears.
3. In the list of printers, select Adobe PDF.
4. To modify the settings for the PDF file you'll create, click the appropriate settings button. The name of this button will vary from application to application, but it's often named Properties or Preferences. After choosing settings, click OK.
5. In the Print dialog box, click Print. The Save PDF File As dialog box appears.
6. From the Save in list, browse to the location where you want to save the file.
7. In the Filename box, enter a name for the PDF document.
8. Click Save. The file is converted to a PostScript file, which is then converted to PDF by Distiller.

Adobe PDF conversion settings

Whichever technique you use to convert a file to PDF, you can specify PDF conversion settings. There are several sets of default Adobe PDF conversion settings to choose from, and each set applies settings for image resolution, font embedding, and more. Each setting strikes a balance between image quality and file size. The settings you choose will depend on how you intend to use the PDF document. For example, if you plan to create a PDF document for general business purposes, such as viewing onscreen and printing to a desktop printer, then you should use the Standard setting, as shown in Exhibit 2-1. If you create a PDF document intended for professional print production, you should use the Press Quality setting.

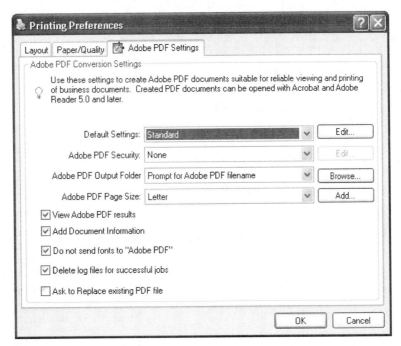

Exhibit 2-1: The Adobe PDF Settings tab in the Printing Preferences dialog box

Font embedding

One option in the Adobe PDF conversion settings is *font embedding*. When a font is embedded in a PDF document, the font will display as it appeared in the original document, even if the document is viewed on (or printed from) a computer that does not have that particular font face. When you embed a font, you can choose to embed every character available with that font, or only a subset made up of the characters actually used in the document. When you embed a subset of the characters, Acrobat stores the font data using a unique name, which ensures that your version of the font is used when the file is printed, rather than a slightly different version of the same font that the printing device might use.

Some fonts cannot be embedded. When a font is not embedded in a document, a similar font is substituted when the PDF file is viewed on a computer that does not have the original font. Acrobat uses a *Multiple Master typeface* to replace any missing fonts. The Multiple Master typeface changes to appear similar to the missing font, and condenses or stretches to fit the space used by the missing font, preventing the document text from reflowing.

Do it!

A-1: Creating a PDF file by using the Print command

Here's how	Here's why
1 Start Microsoft Word	You'll create a PDF file from a document by using the Print command.
Hide the Office Assistant	(If necessary.) Right-click the Office Assistant and select Hide.
2 Open Recipe.doc	(From the current unit folder.) The document contains a recipe flyer. You want to send the document to a coworker for review, and you want to ensure that the layout appears with the same fonts you used, so you'll create a PDF file.
3 Choose **File**, **Print...**	To open the Print dialog box.
4 Under Select Printer, select **Adobe PDF**	
Click **Properties**	
Verify that the Adobe PDF Settings tab is activated	
Verify that **View Adobe PDF results** is checked	You'll specify the default PDF conversion settings to use.
5 From the Default Settings drop-down list, select **Standard**	(If necessary.) A description of the current PDF conversion settings appears above the Default Settings drop-down list.
Observe the description of the Standard settings	You'll use this document for onscreen viewing and printing to a desktop printer, so the Standard setting is appropriate.
6 Click **Edit**	(Located to the right of the Default Settings list.) To open the Standard – PDF Settings dialog box. You can use this dialog box to customize the Standard settings.
In the list on the left, click **Fonts**	To view the font settings.
Verify that Embed all fonts is checked, and click **Cancel**	To close the dialog box without making any changes.
Click **OK**	To return to the Print dialog box.
7 Click **OK**	To open the Save PDF File As dialog box.

8 Navigate to the current unit folder

   Click **Save**   To convert the document to PDF. Acrobat opens
                                                       and displays the document.

9 In Acrobat, close the document

Topic B: Acrobat PDFMaker

This topic covers the following ACE exam objective for Acrobat 8.0 Professional.

#	Objective
3.3	Create a PDF document by using Adobe PDFMaker.

Creating PDF documents with PDFMaker

Explanation

When you install Acrobat 8.0, it automatically adds *PDFMaker* to several applications that you might have installed on your computer. Using PDFMaker, you can convert documents created in any of these applications to PDF format directly from within that application, without using the Print command.

Applications that support PDFMaker

PDFMaker automatically applies to the following applications:

- Autodesk AutoCAD
- Microsoft Access
- Microsoft Excel
- Microsoft Internet Explorer
- Microsoft Outlook
- Microsoft PowerPoint
- Microsoft Publisher
- Microsoft Project
- Microsoft Visio
- Microsoft Word

PDFMaker components

The components that are added to each application might vary. For example, in Microsoft Word, Acrobat 8.0 installs the Acrobat PDFMaker 8.0 and the Acrobat Connect toolbars, shown in Exhibit 2-2, along with the Adobe PDF menu.

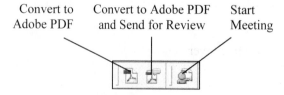

Convert to Adobe PDF   Convert to Adobe PDF and Send for Review   Start Meeting

Exhibit 2-2: The Acrobat PDFMaker 8.0 and Acrobat Connect toolbars

You can customize the settings that PDFMaker uses to generate a PDF file. Choose Adobe PDF, Change Conversion Settings to open the Acrobat PDFMaker dialog box, shown in Exhibit 2-3. In Microsoft Word, this dialog box has four tabs. By default, the Settings tab is active.

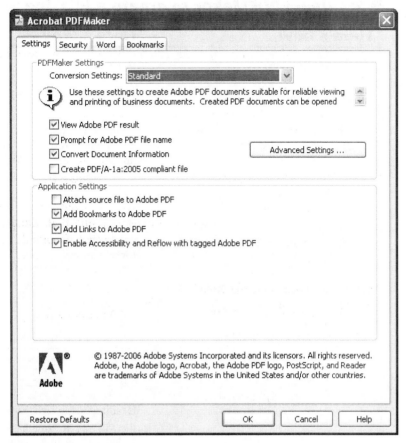

Exhibit 2-3: The Acrobat PDFMaker dialog box in Microsoft Word

The following table describes the options that each tab provides.

Tab	Options
Settings	Change PDFMaker's conversion and application settings.
Security	Control access to the converted PDF document.
Word	Set conversion options for any notes, text boxes, cross-references, tables of contents, footnotes, and endnotes in a Microsoft Word file.
Bookmarks	Specify the headings and styles that you want to convert to bookmarks in the PDF document.

The commands you use to convert a document to PDF using PDFMaker vary depending on the application in use. To convert a Microsoft Office file to a PDF document by using PDFMaker:

1 Open the file in the Microsoft Office application in which it was authored.

2 Select Adobe PDF, Convert to Adobe PDF. (You can also click the Convert to Adobe PDF button on the Adobe PDF toolbar.) The Save Adobe PDF File As dialog box appears.

3 From the Save in list, browse to the location where you want to save the file.

4 In the File name box, type a name.

5 Click Save.

Do it!

B-1: Using PDFMaker to create a PDF file within Word

Here's how	Here's why
1 Switch to Word	If necessary.
Open Memo.doc	From the current unit folder.
2 Choose **Adobe PDF**, **Change Conversion Settings**	To open the Acrobat PDFMaker dialog box. You'll convert the headings in the Word document to bookmarks in the PDF document.
3 Activate the Bookmarks tab	
4 Verify that **Convert Word Headings to Bookmarks** is checked	(Under Bookmark Options.) The headings in the document will automatically become bookmarks for fast access to each heading.
Verify that **Convert Word Styles to Bookmarks** is cleared	
Verify that **Heading 1** is checked	

Type	Bookmark	Level
Heading	☒	1

	Headings 2 through 9 might also be checked, but this document contains only headings with the style Heading 1. All headings defined as level-1 headings will be converted to bookmarks.
Click **OK**	
5 On the Acrobat PDF 8.0 toolbar, click 🅿	(The Convert to Adobe PDF button.) To open the Save Adobe PDF File As dialog box.
6 Save the document as **MyMemo**	(In the current unit folder.) Acrobat PDFMaker converts the document to PDF and opens it in Acrobat.
7 Activate the Bookmarks panel and observe the bookmarks	(In Acrobat.) Acrobat has converted the headings in the Word document into bookmarks.
8 Click the bookmarks	To navigate to each bookmark's associated content.
9 Close the PDF file	
10 Close Microsoft Word	

Topic C: The Create PDF commands

This topic covers the following ACE exam objectives for Acrobat 8.0 Professional.

#	Objective
3.1	List and describe the methods available for creating PDF documents. (Methods include: From a Scanner, from a File)
4.1	List and describe the options available for combining files. (Options include: merging files into a single PDF document, assembling files into a PDF package, creating PDF packages in Microsoft Outlook and Lotus Notes, identifying differences between the Windows and Mac platforms)
4.2	Manage how files are combined and optimized by using the Combine Files dialog box.

Creating PDF documents from within Acrobat

Explanation

You can create PDF documents from a variety of file types by using Acrobat's File, Create PDF commands. You can also access these commands by clicking the Create PDF button on the Tasks toolbar. The following table describes each of the commands in the File, Create PDF submenu.

Create PDF...	Description
From File	Creates a PDF document from a file on your computer. For some file types, the source application might start automatically during the conversion process. You can also access this command by right-clicking a file icon in Windows Explorer and selecting Convert to Adobe PDF.
From Multiple Files	Creates a PDF document from multiple files on your computer. You can combine files of various types, including existing PDF documents.
From Web Page	Creates a PDF document based on one or more Web pages in a site. You can generate a PDF document from a Web site you access via the Internet, or from HTML documents stored on your computer.
From Scanner	Creates a PDF document directly from a document on your scanner.

You can use the Create PDF, From File and Create PDF, From Multiple Files commands to convert the following types of files:

- Adobe PDF
- AutoDesk AutoCAD (.dwg)
- BMP
- Compuserve GIF (.gif)
- HTML
- JPEG
- Microsoft Office (Word, Excel, PowerPoint)
- Microsoft Project
- Microsoft Publisher
- Microsoft Visio
- PCX
- PNG
- PostScript/EPS
- Text
- TIFF

Combining files

If you choose the From Multiple Files command in the Create PDF menu, the Combine Files wizard opens. Using this wizard, you can combine files either as a single PDF document or within a PDF package. Each method has its advantages, as described in the following table.

Combine files	Description
Single PDF document	Combining a group of files into a single PDF document is a good way to ensure that others will see all the files you're including. This method reduces the possibility that other viewers might not open all the files you intended, and makes the files easier to manage because they're all in one document.
PDF package	A PDF package assembles a group of files into a PDF unit. You can view each file independently, but they remain within the package. This method provides more flexibility, because you can add or remove component files without having to find and select specific pages in one document. Also, you can make changes to one of the component files or print specific component files without affecting other files in the package. If you're using Windows, you can also combine Outlook or Lotus Notes e-mail messages and folders in PDF packages by using PDFMaker components within the application.

Combining multiple files to a single PDF file

To combine multiple files to a single PDF file:

1 On the Tasks toolbar, click the Create PDF button and select From Multiple Files. The Combine Files wizard appears, as shown in Exhibit 2-4.

2 Under Choose the files you want to combine, click Add Files. The Add Files dialog box appears.

3 In the dialog box, select one or more files and click Add Files.

4 You can change the order of the files in the Files to combine list in the following ways:

   • Select one or more files and drag them up or down in the list.

   • Select one or more files and click the Move Up and Move Down buttons.

   • Select one or more files, right-click one of the files, and choose Move Up or Move Down.

5 Click Next to move to the next screen in the wizard.

6 Verify that Merge files into a single PDF is selected.

7 Click Create.

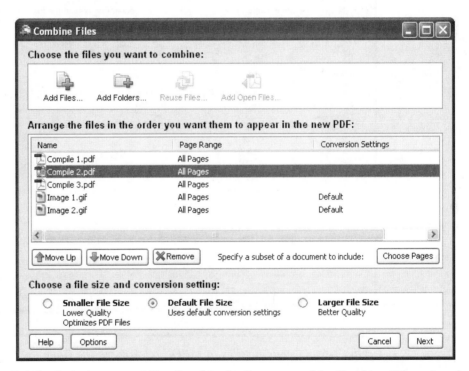

Exhibit 2-4: A group of files listed in the first pane of the Combine Files wizard

Creating a PDF package

To create a PDF package:

1 On the Tasks toolbar, click the Create PDF button and select From Multiple Files. The Combine Files wizard appears.

2 At the top of the dialog box, click Add Files. The Add Files dialog box appears.

3 In the dialog box, select one or more files and click Add Files.

4 Set the order of the documents by dragging or using the Move Up or Move Down buttons.

5 Click Next to move to the next screen in the wizard.

6 Select Assemble files into a PDF Package, as shown in Exhibit 2-5.

7 Under Select Cover Sheet, select either Use Adobe template or Use first document.

8 Click Create.

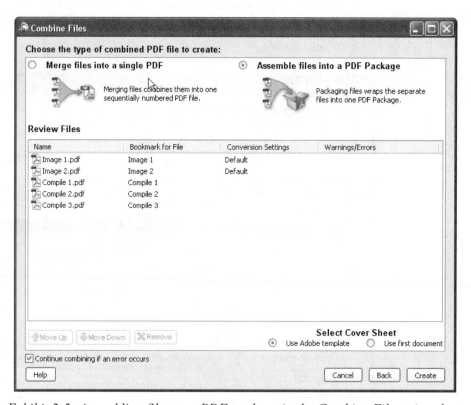

Exhibit 2-5: Assembling files as a PDF package in the Combine Files wizard

Do it!

C-1: Combining multiple documents in a PDF package

Here's how	Here's why
1 Verify that Acrobat is the active program	
2 Click the **Create PDF** button	(In the Tasks toolbar.) To display the drop-down list. You can also choose File, Create PDF, From Multiple Files.
Choose **From Multiple Files...**	To open the Combine Files wizard.
3 Under Choose the files you want to combine, click **Add Files...**	Add Files...
	To open the Add Files dialog box.
Navigate to the current unit folder	
4 Click **Compile 1.pdf**	
Press and hold ⌜SHIFT⌝	
Click **Image 2.gif**	To select the Compile 1, Compile 2, Compile 3, Image 1, and Image 2 files.
Click **Add Files**	**Arrange the files** Name Compile 1.pdf Compile 2.pdf Compile 3.pdf Image 1.gif Image 2.gif
	The files are added to the list. Acrobat will combine them in this order. You'll Move the two image files to the top of the list.
5 In the Files to Combine list, select **Image 1.gif** and **Image 2.gif**	
Drag the selected files above Compile 1.pdf, as shown	**Arrange the files** Name Image 1.gif Image 2.gif Compile 1.pdf Compile 2.pdf Compile 3.pdf

6	Click **Next**	A dialog box might appear, displaying information about working with pictures.
	Select **Assemble files into a PDF Package**	**Assemble files into a PDF Package** Packaging files wraps the separate files into one PDF Package.
7	Click **Create**	
8	Click **Save**	
	Save the document as **My compilation**	(In the current unit folder.) The document opens in Acrobat.
9	View the document in Single Page layout	Click the Single Page layout button in the Page Display toolbar.
	Browse through the new document	The files are compiled in the order you specified.
10	Close the document	

Converting HTML documents to PDF

Explanation

You can also convert HTML documents to PDF. You can convert Web pages and sites that you access online or HTML documents stored on your computer. One benefit of converting a Web page to PDF is that the PDF version can produce a better-quality print. For example, the edges of Web pages often get cut off when printed to letter-sized paper, and a browser's print function can't always render graphics correctly. Converting Web pages to PDF shrinks the content to fit to the paper size you specify, ensuring that the content will print in its entirety. Also, if you want someone to review a site and provide feedback, you can convert all the site files to a single PDF document that others could review using Acrobat.

Acrobat and Internet Explorer

When you install Acrobat 8.0 Professional, it also adds a toolbar and button to Internet Explorer 5.01 and later, which you can use to convert the current Web page to a PDF document. Because Web content changes, you might want to save a Web page to PDF to ensure that you'll be able to view that content later.

The Create PDF from Web Page command

If you want to convert multiple Web pages or even an entire Web site to a single PDF document, choose Create PDF, From Web Page. This opens the Create PDF from Web Page dialog box, shown in Exhibit 2-6. Each Web page is converted to one or more PDF document pages. Any links on the original Web pages still function as links within the converted PDF document. Clicking a link in the PDF document downloads and converts the linked Web page and adds it to the end of the PDF document.

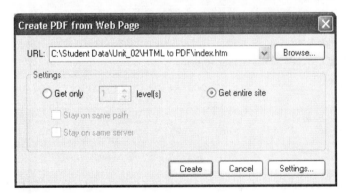

Exhibit 2-6: The Create PDF from Web Page dialog box

To convert Web pages to PDF:

1   On the Tasks toolbar, click the Create PDF button and select From Web Page. The Create PDF from Web Page dialog box appears.

2   In the URL box, enter the Web address or file location of the HTML content you want to convert:

  • Enter the Web address of the site or page you want to convert.

  • Click Browse and navigate to the HTML file on your computer you want to convert.

3   Under Settings, specify if you want to convert the entire site or only a specified number of the site's levels.

4   Click Settings to open the Web Page Conversion Settings dialog box, shown in Exhibit 2-7. Specify the PDF settings you want to use.

5   Activate the Page Layout tab to specify layout options, as shown in Exhibit 2-8. For example, because Web pages are often designed to be wider than tall, you might want to specify a Landscape orientation.

6   Click Create to create the PDF file.

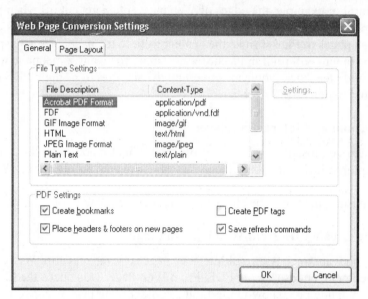

Exhibit 2-7: The Web Page Conversion Settings dialog box

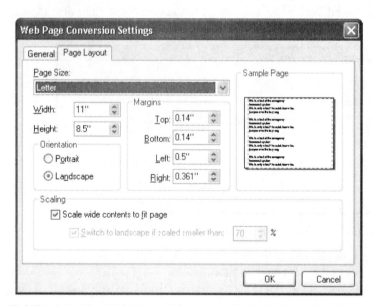

Exhibit 2-8: The Web Page Conversion Settings Page Layout options

Viewing PDF documents on the Web

You can control how you view PDF documents that you access on the Web. You can set PDF documents to open directly in your browser, or in a separate Acrobat window.

To specify how PDF documents open on your system:

1   Choose Edit, Preferences to open the Preferences dialog box.

2   In the Categories list, select Internet.

3   Under Web Browser Options, check Display PDF in browser if you want to open PDF documents directly in your browser, or clear this option if you want to open PDF files in a separate Acrobat window.

4   Click OK.

This setting affects only how you view PDF documents on your computer. It does not control how PDF documents that you generate will appear for other users. Users who open PDF files within an Acrobat window will be able to use all of Acrobat's features to view and navigate the document. However, those who open PDF files within their browser will have only a subset of Acrobat's tools. Therefore, you should include links and bookmarks that will help online viewers navigate the PDF file more easily.

For example, an online viewer can't use the browser's Back and Forward buttons to navigate the PDF document pages, so Acrobat's page navigation buttons are added to the browser window, as shown in Exhibit 2-9. A subset of Acrobat's tools will appear in the browser window as well, including the File, Basic, and Zoom toolbars.

Exhibit 2-9: Navigation buttons that appear in a Web browser

Controlling how a PDF document downloads

When you create a PDF document, you can set the PDF to download one page at a time so that online users can begin viewing the document right away, rather than having to wait for the download to complete before any pages become visible. You can specify this page-at-a-time downloading by enabling the Fast Web View option:

1   Choose Edit, Preferences to open the Preferences dialog box.

2   In the Categories list, select Documents.

3   Under Save Settings, select Save As optimizes for Fast Web View. (This is the default setting.)

4   Click OK.

5   Choose File, Save As and specify a name and location for the file.

Finally, you should also embed fonts when you generate a PDF document that you'll distribute via the Web, to ensure that users will be able to view the text as designed.

C-2: Converting HTML documents to PDF

Here's how	Here's why
1 Click the **Create PDF** button	
Select **From Web Page...**	To open the Create PDF from Web Page dialog box.
2 Click **Browse**	The Select File to Open dialog box appears.
In the current unit folder, open the HTML to PDF subfolder	
Select **index.htm**	This file is the Web site's home page.
3 Click **Select**	To return to the Create PDF from Web Page dialog box. You'll generate bookmarks for all the Web pages in the site.
4 Click **Settings...**	To open the Web Page Conversion Settings dialog box.
Verify that **Create Bookmarks** is checked	To help keep the Web pages from being scaled down too much to fit to the width of letter-sized paper, you'll use landscape orientation.
5 Activate the Page Layout tab	To display the Page Layout options.
6 Under Orientation, select **Landscape**	
Click **OK**	To return to the Create PDF from Web Page dialog box. You'll include all the Web site pages in the PDF document.
7 Select **Get entire site**	
8 Click **Create**	To generate a PDF document based on the HTML file. An alert dialog box appears, indicating that this operation might take a long time.
Click **Yes**	To indicate that you want to proceed. The PDF document appears, and bookmarks for each Web page appear in the Bookmarks panel.
9 Click [⟷]	(On the Select & Zoom toolbar.) To display the document pages at Fit Width magnification.
10 Click each bookmark	To view each Web page.
Return to the first page and click the links on the Web page	To navigate the Web site pages within the PDF document.

11	Save the PDF file as **My Web site**	In the current unit folder.
12	Close the file	

Unit summary: Converting documents to PDF

Topic A
In this topic, you learned how to **convert a document to PDF** using the **Adobe PDF printer**. You also learned how to adjust **conversion settings**, and you learned about **embedding fonts** in a PDF document to ensure that a user can view the text in a PDF document as originally designed.

Topic B
In this topic, you learned how to **convert Microsoft Office documents** from within Microsoft Office applications by using **PDFMaker**.

Topic C
In this topic, you learned how to use the **Create PDF commands** in Acrobat, and you learned how to create PDF documents from **multiple files** and from **Web pages**.

Independent practice activity

In this activity, you'll convert a Word document to a PDF file containing bookmarks. You'll also convert a document to PDF by using the Adobe PDF Printer. Finally, you'll combine multiple files to a single PDF file.

1 In Microsoft Word, open Word to PDF practice.doc from the current unit folder.

2 This document contains a custom style named "Team member." Change the PDF conversion settings so that only text with the style "Team member" is converted to a bookmark. (*Hint*: Clear both check boxes above the Element listing before selecting the style you want.)

3 Convert the document to PDF and save it as **My Word to practice PDF** (in the current unit folder).

4 In Acrobat, test the bookmarks.

5 Close the file in Acrobat and close Microsoft Word.

6 In WordPad, open Outlander logo.rtf from the current unit folder.

7 Convert the document to PDF by using the Standard conversion setting, and save it in the current unit folder as **My Outlander logo**. (*Hint*: Use the Adobe PDF Printer.)

8 Close the Acrobat file and close WordPad.

9 Combine the two PDF documents you've created into a PDF package so that the new document begins with the My Outlander logo file.

10 Save the document as **My compilation practice** in the current unit folder.

11 Close all files.

Review questions

1 Which of these statements are true regarding font embedding? (Choose all that apply.)

   A When you embed a font, you can choose to embed every character available with that font, or only a subset made up of the characters actually used in the document.

   B When you embed a font, all characters available with that font are always embedded.

   C When a font is embedded in a PDF file, the font will be displayed properly on any computer.

   D When a font is embedded in a PDF file, the font will be displayed properly only on computers on which the font is installed.

2 You've received a PDF file that includes type formatted in a font not installed on your computer. The font was not embedded in the PDF file. How will the type appear?

   A The type won't appear at all in the file because it's not available.

   B The type will appear similarly to the original font formatting, with a Multiple Master typeface replacing the original font.

   C The computer's default font will be used to display the type.

   D The type will appear using the original font.

3 You've created a file in a page layout application, and the file uses that application's standard file format. You want to convert it to PDF. What should you do?

   A Convert the file directly by using Distiller.

   B Choose the page layout application's Print command and select the Adobe PDF printer to generate a PostScript file that Distiller will convert to PDF.

   C In Acrobat, choose File, Open As PDF.

   D Use Distiller to convert the file to PostScript format, and then use the Adobe PDF printer to convert the PostScript file to PDF.

4 You've created a Microsoft Word file that has headings formatted by using styles. When you convert the file to PDF, and want to generate bookmarks for the document headings, what should you do?

   A Generate the PDF file, open the PDF file in Acrobat, and manually create the bookmarks.

   B In Word, choose Format, Styles, select the heading style, and check Generate Bookmarks.

   C In Word, choose Adobe PDF, Change Conversion Settings; then activate the Bookmarks tab and check Convert Word Styles to Bookmarks.

   D In Word, choose Tools, Options, activate the PDF Settings tag, and check Convert Styles to Bookmarks.

5 True or false? PDFMaker automatically applies to all Microsoft Office applications, as well as many other Microsoft applications.

6 You've created a Microsoft Word file and want to specify conversion options for the document's footnotes and endnotes. In the Acrobat PDFMaker dialog box, which tab should you use?

A Settings

B Security

C Word

D Bookmarks

7 You've created a Microsoft Word file that you want to convert to a PDF file capable of high quality print production/separation. In the Acrobat PDFMaker dialog box, which tab should you use to specify the conversion setting?

A Settings

B Security

C Word

D Bookmarks

8 True or false? When you use the File, Create PDF, From File command, the source application might start automatically during the conversion process.

9 You have a PDF file, a Microsoft Word file, and an HTML file that you want to combine as a single PDF file. What should you do?

A Convert the Word and HTML files to individual PDF files, and then combine them by using the Pages panel in Acrobat.

B In Word, use PDFMaker to combine all three files to a single PDF file.

C Convert the Word and HTML files to individual PDF files, and then open them in Acrobat and choose File, Combine Files.

D In Acrobat's Tasks toolbar, click the Create PDF button and select From Multiple Files.

10 In the Combine Files wizard, how can you change the order of the files you're combining? (Choose all that apply).

A Press and hold Ctrl; then press the Up or Down arrow keys.

B Drag the files up or down in the list.

C Right-click one of the files and choose Move Up or Move Down.

D Click the Move Up or Move Down buttons.

11 What's the most efficient way to generate a single PDF file from multiple documents?

    A Create a PDF file for each document, then use the Pages palette to combine the files.

    B In Windows Explorer, select all the files you want to include and drag them to the Acrobat icon on the taskbar.

    C On the Tasks toolbar, click the Create PDF button and select From Multiple Files.

    D On the Tasks toolbar, click the Create PDF button and select From File; then press Ctrl, click each file you want to include, and click Open.

12 When a user accesses a PDF file via a Web browser, how can the user navigate between the pages? (Choose all that apply.)

    A By clicking any available navigation links in the PDF file.

    B By clicking the Web browser's Back and Forward buttons.

    C By using the Web Browser's Go, View, or History menu.

    D By using Acrobat's page navigation buttons.

Unit 3

Modifying PDF documents

Unit time: 60 minutes

Complete this unit, and you'll know how to:

A Arrange, move, delete, and extract PDF document pages.

B Edit text, add headers and footers, and number pages in a PDF document.

C Move PDF content into files created in other programs.

D Reduce PDF file size.

Topic A: Modifying document pages

This topic covers the following ACE exam objectives for Acrobat 8.0 Professional.

#	Objective
5.1	Explain how to modify PDF documents by selecting options from the Document menu.
5.4	Rearrange and number pages by using the Pages panel.

Manipulating pages

Explanation

Acrobat 8.0 makes it easy to manipulate pages in a PDF document. You can arrange pages within a PDF document or move pages from one document to another. You can also extract individual pages and save them in a new document or delete unnecessary pages when necessary.

Arranging pages in the Pages panel

You can rearrange the pages in a PDF document by using the Pages panel. Making the navigation pane wider displays the Pages panel thumbnails in more than one row. To adjust its width, drag the right edge of the navigation pane, as shown in Exhibit 3-1.

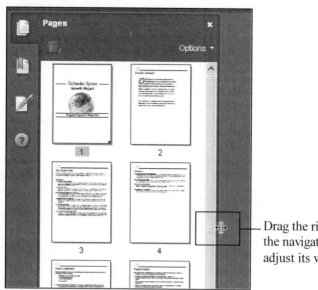

Drag the right edge of the navigation pane to adjust its width.

Exhibit 3-1: Adjusting the width of the Pages panel

To move a page within a document, activate the Pages panel, and then drag a page thumbnail to a new location. You can also select and move multiple pages simultaneously. To select a range of pages, press and hold Shift and select the first and last page thumbnails in the range. To select multiple pages that are not in a sequential range, press and hold Ctrl and click each thumbnail. As you drag page thumbnails, a vertical bar indicates where the pages will be placed when you release the mouse button.

Do it!

A-1: Arranging PDF document pages

Here's how	Here's why
1 Open Arrange pages.pdf	From the current unit folder.
Save the file as **My Arrange pages**	(In the current unit folder.) You'll observe the pages as thumbnails in the Pages panel.
2 Activate the Pages panel	In the navigation pane, click the Pages icon.
Point to the right edge of the pane	
	(You'll widen the navigation pane.) The pointer changes, indicating you can drag to resize the pane.
Drag to the right	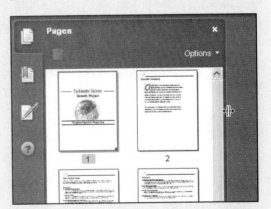
	To widen the pane so that the page thumbnails appear in two columns. You'll move page 5 so that it appears before page 3.

3 Drag the page 5 thumbnail to the
   left of the page 3 thumbnail, as
   shown

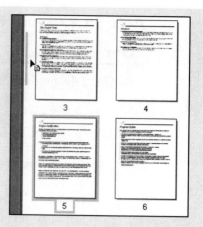

The page you dragged is now page 3.

4 Save the document

Moving pages between documents

Explanation

You can also move pages from one document to another. With both documents open, drag page thumbnails from the Pages panel of one document to the desired location in the Pages panel of the other document.

To move or copy pages between documents:

1 Open the documents.

2 Choose Window, Tile, Vertically, or press Shift+Ctrl+L. This allows you to view both documents side by side, as shown in Exhibit 3-2.

3 Activate the Pages panel in the navigation pane of each document.

4 To copy a page from one document to another (leaving the original page intact), select the page thumbnail of one document and drag it to the desired location of the other document. To move a page (and remove it from its original location), hold down the Ctrl key while you drag.

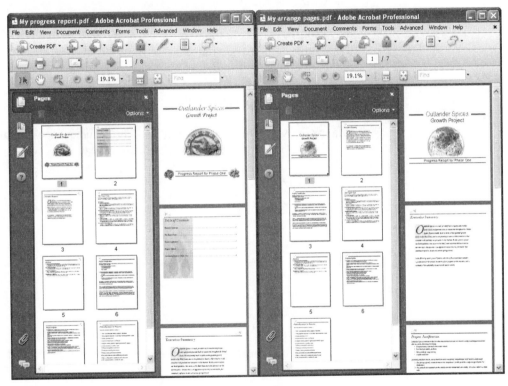

Exhibit 3-2: Viewing two documents side-by-side

You can also move pages between documents by using the Insert Pages command, from either the Document menu or the Pages panel's Options menu. However, the Insert Pages command inserts all pages from the specified document into the current document. You can't use the Insert Pages command to insert only selected pages from a file.

A-2: Moving pages between PDF documents

Here's how	Here's why
1 Open Progress report.pdf	(From the current unit folder.) You'll copy the cover page from the Progress report to the My arrange pages document.
2 Save the file as **My Progress report**	In the current unit folder.
3 Choose **Window**, **Tile**, **Vertically**	To position the two documents side by side.
4 Show the Pages panel in both documents	If necessary.
5 Drag the page 1 thumbnail from My Progress report to the beginning of the My Arrange pages document	To add the cover page from the My Progress report document to the My Arrange pages document.
6 Close My Progress report.pdf	
7 Maximize My Arrange pages.pdf	The document now contains two versions of the cover page.

Deleting and replacing pages

Explanation

You can delete unwanted pages or replace them with pages from other documents by using either menu commands or page thumbnails.

Deleting pages

To delete pages from a PDF document:

1   Open the document.
2   Choose Document, Delete Pages. The Delete Pages dialog box appears.
3   In the From and To boxes, enter the range of pages that you want to delete.
4   Click OK.

You can also delete document pages by selecting page thumbnails in the Pages panel and pressing Delete.

Replacing pages

To replace the pages of a PDF document with pages from another PDF document:

1   Choose Document, Replace Pages.
2   Select the file that contains the replacement pages.
3   Click Select. The Replace Pages dialog box appears, as shown in Exhibit 3-3.
4   Under Original, enter the range of pages you want to replace.
5   Under Replacement, specify the pages that will replace the pages in the original file. (The range of replacement pages is calculated automatically.)
6   Click OK. A confirmation dialog box appears. Click Yes.

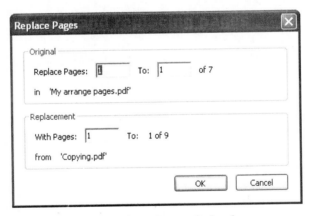

Exhibit 3-3: The Replace Pages dialog box

Do it!

A-3: Deleting PDF document pages

Here's how	Here's why
1 In the Pages panel, click the page 2 thumbnail	This is the old cover page, which you no longer need.
2 Press (DELETE)	A warning dialog box appears.
3 Click **OK**	To delete the page.
4 Save the document	

Extracting pages

Explanation

You can extract pages from a PDF document and save those pages as a separate PDF file. This is useful when you want to distribute part of a document to people who don't need to see the entire document. You can choose to extract a page or several pages while leaving the original document intact, or you can choose to delete them from the original document. You can also choose to extract non-sequential pages.

To extract pages from a document:

1 Choose Document, Extract Pages. The Extract pages dialog box appears, as shown in Exhibit 3-4.

2 Enter the range of pages you want to extract.

- If you want to delete the extracted pages from the original document, check Delete Pages After Extracting.

- If you want to extract each page as a separate document, check Extract Pages As Separate Files.

3 Click OK. The pages are extracted to a new PDF document.

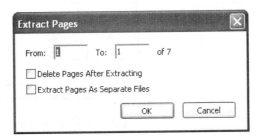

Exhibit 3-4: The Extract Pages dialog box

You can also select the pages you want to extract in the Pages panel, then right-click one of the selected thumbnails and select Extract Pages.

A-4:   Extracting PDF document pages

Here's how	Here's why
1 Open the Pages panel	If necessary.
2 Click the page 4 thumbnail	You'll extract pages from this document and save them as a separate document.
Hold down CTRL and click the page 5 thumbnail	To select both thumbnails.
Release CTRL	
3 Right-click either page's thumbnail	To open the shortcut menu.
Choose **Extract Pages...**	

Extract Pages

From: 4   To: 5   of 7

☐ Delete Pages After Extracting
☐ Extract Pages As Separate Files

[OK] [Cancel]

	To open the Extract Pages dialog box.
4 Verify that Delete Pages After Extracting is cleared	You'll save the selected pages to a new file without deleting them from the original file.
5 Verify that Extract Pages As Separate Files is cleared	You'll save the two pages as a single PDF document, rather than two separate PDF documents.
Click **OK**	The extracted pages open as a new PDF document.
6 Save the file as **Extracted pages**	In the current unit folder.
7 Save and close all documents	

Topic B: Modifying content

This topic covers the following ACE exam objectives for Acrobat 8.0 Professional.

#	Objective
4.3	Incorporate headers, footers, watermarks, and backgrounds to a PDF document.
5.1	Explain how to modify PDF documents by selecting options from the Document menu.
5.2	Given a tool on the Advanced Editing toolbar, explain how to use that tool. (Tools include: Link, Crop, TouchUp Text, TouchUp Object, Movie, Sound)
5.4	Rearrange and number pages by using the Pages panel.

Editing content

Explanation

You can use Acrobat to modify the content of PDF documents. For example, you can edit text, add headers and footers, or modify page numbering. Keep in mind that extensive PDF edits can be tedious and can cause layout problems. If you need to make major editorial changes or layout changes, you should always make the changes in the document's source program, such as Microsoft Word, and then output a new copy to PDF.

The Advanced Editing toolbar

To modify content, you need to work with the Advanced Editing tools. You can select a tool by choosing one from the Tools, Advanced Editing submenu. You can also open the Advanced Editing toolbar (shown in Exhibit 3-5) by either choosing Tools, Advanced Editing, Show Advanced Editing toolbar, or by right-clicking on a blank area in one of the visible toolbars and choosing Advanced Editing.

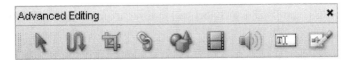

Exhibit 3-5: The Advanced Editing toolbar

The following table describes each of the tools in the toolbar.

Tool	Description
	Use the Select Object tool to perform simple editing tasks for most page objects. You can modify the properties, size, and location of objects. To use the tool, click on the page to view editable objects, and then make the changes.
	Use the Article tool to create and modify article boxes. An *article* is an electronic thread that a PDF author may define within the PDF. Articles allow authors to direct readers through specific content similar to the way readers sometimes navigate a newspaper. To use the tool, drag to create a box around the content you want to include in the article.
	Use the Crop tool to crop pages. To use the tool, drag to create a box around the area you want to remain visible. Areas outside the crop box will be hidden. Double-click in the box to crop the page.
	Use the Link tool to create links. To use the tool, drag to create a box around the area you want to be the link trigger. In the dialog box, select the type of link you want to create.
	Use the 3D tool to create a new area for a 3D object. To use the tool, drag to create a box for the 3D object. In the dialog box, define the settings for the new 3D object.
	Use the Movie tool to add movie files. To use the tool, drag to create a box for the movie file. In the dialog box, navigate to the movie file you want to use and set basic movie attributes.
	Use the Sound tool to define a trigger area that activates sound. To use the tool, drag to create a box around the area you want to be the sound trigger. In the dialog box, navigate to the sound file you want to use, and set basic attributes.
	Use the TouchUp Text tool to make minor text edits. To use the tool, click the text you want to edit to place the insertion point, and then make the changes.
	Use the TouchUp Object tool to make minor object edits. To use the tool, click the object you want to modify, and then make the changes. You can also right-click an object to perform other changes.

The TouchUp Text tool

You can use the TouchUp Text tool to select, insert, delete, or copy text in PDF documents. However, if the original fonts used in the document are not available on your computer, a dialog box will appear indicating that a substitute font will be used, which could create additional font dependencies in the document. In addition to editing text, you can also modify text color, word spacing, character spacing, baseline offset, or margins.

To edit PDF document text:

1. Open the document.
2. Choose Tools, Advanced Editing, TouchUp Text Tool or select the TouchUp Text tool from the Advanced Editing toolbar.
3. Edit the text.
   - Click to place the insertion point and type to add text.
   - Select text and type to replace the selected text.
   - Select text and press Delete to remove text.

Do it!

B-1: Editing PDF document text

Here's how	Here's why
1 Open My Progress report.pdf	From the current unit folder.
2 View page 3 at Fit Width magnification	You'll update the number of kiosks mentioned in this text.
3 Right-click a blank area in one of the toolbars and select **Advanced Editing**	To open the Advanced Editing toolbar. The toolbar appears as a floating toolbar.
4 Click	(The TouchUp Text tool.) You'll use this tool to update some text.
5 Click any text on page 3	To activate the tool. The status bar indicates that Acrobat is loading system fonts. (A dialog box might appear indicating that the original font is not available on your computer. Click OK to close the dialog box.)
6 Select the word **twenty**, as shown	*exotic spices and gourmet fo* *States. We have* twenty *kiosk*
Type **thirty**	To replace the selected text.
Observe the right edge of the paragraph	Because the word you replaced is nearly the same length as the new word, the line length is about the same as it was originally.
7 Save the document	

Type formatting options

Explanation
You can change PDF document type formatting, even for embedded text that uses a font that's not installed on your computer. You can use the TouchUp Properties dialog box, shown in Exhibit 3-6, to adjust formatting.

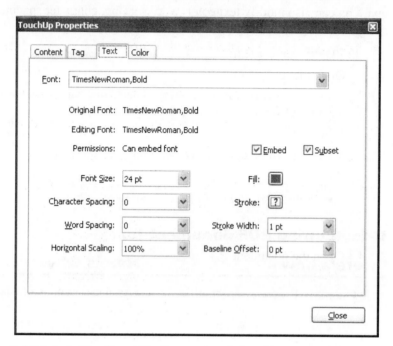

Exhibit 3-6: The TouchUp Properties dialog box

The following table describes the options available on the Text tab of the TouchUp Properties dialog box.

Option	Description
Font	Applies a font.
Permissions	Displays the document's permissions to embed fonts: • **Can embed.** You can use both the Embed and Subset options to embed or unembed document fonts. • **Can embed for print and preview only.** You can use the Embed option for printing and previewing. • **Cannot embed.** You can't use the Embed or Subset options. • **Can embed font for editing.** You can use the Subset option but not the Embed option. • **No system font available.** You can't use the Embed or Subset options.
Embed	Specifies whether to embed fonts in the document. To edit a PDF document, the font used in the document must be installed on your computer or embedded in the document.
Subset	Specifies whether to embed a subset of a font in your document. The subset includes only the characters used in the document, rather than the entire family of variants that are typically bundled with a font.

Option	Description
Font Size	Specifies the font size.
Character Spacing	Applies uniform spacing between characters in the selected text.
Word Spacing	Applies uniform spacing between words in the selected text.
Horizontal Scaling	Specifies the proportion between the height and the width of the selected text.
Fill	Specifies a color with which to fill the selected text.
Stroke	Specifies a color with which to outline the selected text.
Stroke Width	Specifies the width of the text outline.
Baseline Offset	Specifies how far text is moved from its baseline.

To change fonts, styles, and other text characteristics:

1   Open the document.
2   Choose Tools, Advanced Editing, TouchUp Text Tool, or select the TouchUp Text tool from the Advanced Editing toolbar.
3   Highlight the text that you want to format.
4   Right-click in the selected text area and choose Properties. The TouchUp Properties dialog box appears.
5   Select the formatting options you want.
6   Click Close.

Do it!

B-2: Formatting PDF document text

Here's how	Here's why
1 With the TouchUp Text tool, select **Executive Summary**	(The green heading above the first paragraph.) You'll apply italic formatting to the heading.
2 Right-click the selected text	To open the shortcut menu.
Select **Properties...**	To open the TouchUp Properties dialog box.
3 Verify that the Text tab is activated	The text already uses bold formatting. You'll add italic formatting.
4 From the Font drop-down list, select **TimesNewRoman, BoldItalic**	(Your version of Times New Roman, BoldItalic might have a slightly different name.) To apply the bold-italicized version of Times New Roman.
5 Click **Close**	
Observe the text you formatted	The heading now uses italic formatting.
6 Close the Advanced Editing toolbar	
7 Select the Hand tool	To ensure that you won't inadvertently modify document text as you work on the next activities.
8 Save the file	

Headers and footers

Explanation

Headers and footers provide users with consistent content across a range of pages or all the pages in a document. A *header* is information that appears at the top of each page, and a *footer* is information at the bottom of each page. You can create headers and footers to provide information such as the date, page titles, or page numbers. To add a header or footer to a document, use the Add Header and Footer dialog box, shown in Exhibit 3-7.

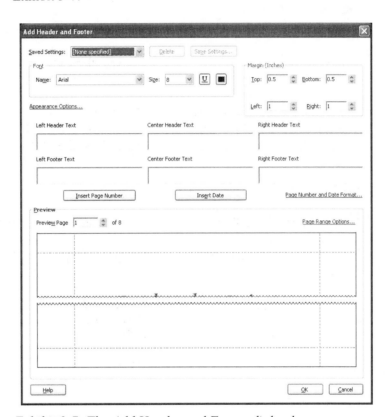

Exhibit 3-7: The Add Header and Footer dialog box

To create a header or footer:

1   Choose Document, Header & Footer, Add to open the Add Header and Footer dialog box.

2   Click one of the six header or footer boxes to indicate whether the header or footer should appear on the left, right, or center of the header or footer area.

3   Enter your header or footer content.

- To add page numbers, click Insert Page Number.
- To add a date, click Insert Date. (You can format page numbers and dates by clicking the Page Number and Date format link on the right side.)
- To enter your own custom text, type directly in the boxes.

4   To format the header or footer, select it, and select from the formatting options at the top of the dialog box.

5   To specify the pages on which you want the header or footer to appear, click the Page Range Options link on the right side.

6   Click OK.

Do it!   **B-3:   Adding headers and footers**

Here's how	Here's why
1 Choose **Document**, **Header & Footer**, **Add...**	To open the Header and Footer dialog box. You'll add a header to the document.
2 In the Left Header Text box, type **Outlander Spices**	Left Header Text Outlander Spices| Left Footer Text
	The top box under Preview shows the location of the header on the page.
3 Click to place the insertion point in the Center Header Text box	
Click **Insert Date**	The current date appears in the preview pane showing the day and month. You want the date to also show the year.
4 Select the date code in the Center Header Text box	Center Header Text <<m/d>>
Press (DELETE)	To remove it.
5 Click the **Page Number and Date Format** link	Right Footer Text Page Number and Date Format...
	To open the Page Number and Date Format dialog box.
From the Date Format list, select **mm/dd/yyyy**	
Click **OK**	
6 Click to place the insertion point in the Center Header Text box	
Click **Insert Date**	To add the date using the format you selected.

7	Click to place the insertion point in the Right Header Text box	
8	Click the **Page Number and Date Format** link	To open the Page Number and Date Format dialog box.
	From the Page Number Format list, select **1 of n**	
	Click **OK**	
9	Click **Insert Page Number**	To add page numbers to the header.
10	Click the **Page Range Options** link	To open the Page Range Options dialog box.
	Verify that All Pages is selected, and click **OK**	
11	Click **OK**	To apply the header to the document.
12	Save and close the document	

Numbering pages

Explanation
By default, Acrobat identifies pages sequentially, beginning with 1. Therefore, a document's first page is page 1, the second page is page 2, and so on. This page numbering is shown in the Pages panel and in the Page Navigation toolbar. However, there might be another set of page numbers that appear on the document pages themselves. For example, page numbers might have been added to the document pages in the source application. The page numbers that appear on the document pages might not match the page numbers that Acrobat assigns. For example, if the first page is a title page and the second page is a table of contents, the third page might be numbered as page 1. However, Acrobat would identify that page as page 3, because it's the third page in the document.

You can use the Page Numbering dialog box to customize how Acrobat numbers the pages, to match the page numbers on the document pages.

To renumber pages:

1 In the navigation pane, activate the Pages panel.

2 Choose Options, Number Pages. The Page Numbering dialog box appears, as shown in Exhibit 3-8.

3 Under Pages, enter the range of pages to which you want to apply numbering.

4 To select a new numbering sequence, select Begin new section. (You can also extend the numbering, if any, used in the previous set of pages.)

5 From the Style list, select a numbering format. You can also customize the numbering style by adding a prefix to the selected style. For example, you can prefix page numbers with the name of the document.

6 Click OK.

Exhibit 3-8: The Page Numbering dialog box

Do it!

B-4:   Synchronizing page numbering

Here's how	Here's why
1 Open Numbering.pdf	(From the current unit folder.) You want to make the page numbers in Acrobat match those in the original document.
Save the file as **My Numbering**	In the current unit folder.
2 Open the Pages panel	
3 Scroll to the bottom of the first page and observe the page numbering	The lowercase Roman numeral i appears at the bottom of the page.
4 Navigate to the fourth page	In the Pages panel, click the Page 4 icon.
Observe the page numbering	The first two pages of the document are numbered with Roman numerals. The fourth page of the document is numbered as page 2 even though it's the fourth page in the document. You'll change the Acrobat file to match this page numbering.
5 In the Pages panel, Select **Options, Number Pages...**	To open the Page Numbering dialog box.
6 Under Pages, select **From**	You'll change the numbering of a range of pages, rather than the entire document.
In the From: box, enter **1**	
In the To: box, enter **2**	
7 Under Numbering, verify that **Begin new section** is selected	
From the Style list, select **i, ii, iii, ...**	To apply lowercase roman numerals.
Verify that the Start box is set to 1	To begin numbering this section with page 1, but using Roman numerals.
Click **OK**	The first two pages are numbered i and ii.
8 Observe the Pages panel thumbnails	The numbers below each page thumbnail show the new page numbering.
Navigate to the second page	(In the Pages panel, click the Page 2 icon.) The second page uses a Roman numeral.

9	Navigate to the sixth page	In the Pages panel, click the Page 6 icon.
	In the Page Navigation toolbar, observe the page number boxes	
		The page numbering matches the page numbering that appears on the document pages. The toolbar also displays the absolute page numbering within parentheses.
10	In the Page Navigation toolbar, enter **(4)**	To navigate to the fourth page based on its absolute page number. Typing a page number within parentheses navigates to the absolute page number. This is the fourth page in the document, although the number on the page itself is 2.
11	Save and close the document	

Topic C: Moving PDF content to other programs

Explanation

You might want to use content from a PDF document in another program. For example, say you have a PDF document and you need to work with its content in a text editor. If you don't have an original version of the file in its source application, you can convert the PDF document to a text file. Or, you might want to copy just a portion of content from a PDF document for use in another file. You can copy text, graphics, and tables from PDF documents and paste them into other programs.

Copying content from a PDF document

If you want to copy some text from a PDF document into another program, you can select the text or object by using the Select tool and choose Edit, Copy to copy it to the Clipboard. Next, open a file in the program where you want to add the text and choose Edit, Paste.

To copy a graphic from a PDF document and paste it into another program:

1 With the Select tool, click the graphic you want to copy.

2 Copy the graphic.

- Choose Edit, Copy.
- Right-click the graphic and select Copy Image to Clipboard.
- On the graphic, click the Copy Image to Clipboard button that appears.

3 Open the file in which you want to add the graphic.

4 Choose Edit, Paste to insert a copy of the graphic.

You can also export all graphics from a PDF document by choosing Advanced, Export All Images.

Converting from PDF to other file formats

After you convert a document from its source application to a PDF document, you can't convert the PDF version back to the original format of its source application. For example, if you create a PDF document from an InDesign file, you can't directly convert the PDF version back to an InDesign document. However, you can save a PDF document to several file types, including Encapsulated PostScript (EPS), HTML, JPEG, RTF, Microsoft Word, text, or XML. To save a PDF document to another format, choose File, Save As. From the Save As Type list, select the format you want to use and click Save.

Do it!

C-1: Copying a graphic to another program

Here's how	Here's why
1 Open Copy graphic.pdf	(From the current unit folder.) You'll copy the graphic from the first page to a Word file.
2 On the Select & Zoom toolbar, click	The Select tool.
Click the graphic	(The large graphic of a plate of food.) To select it.
3 Choose **Edit**, **Copy**	To copy the graphic.
4 Start Microsoft Word	
Create a new blank document	If necessary.
5 Choose **Edit**, **Paste**	To paste the graphic at the top of the Word document.
6 Press ⏎ENTER twice	To move the insertion point down.
7 Save the file as **Issues**	In the current unit folder.
8 Close Word	
9 Return to Acrobat and close the document	

Topic D: Optimizing PDF file size

This topic covers the following ACE exam objective for Acrobat 8.0 Professional.

#	Objective
5.5	Given a scenario, optimize the size of a PDF document by using the PDF Optimizer.

The PDF Optimizer

Explanation

When you use Acrobat Distiller to create a PDF document, you can specify options that impact the PDF file size, such as font embedding and image compression settings. However, no matter how a PDF document was created, you can use Acrobat's PDF Optimizer to *optimize* its file size, achieving the best balance between file size and document properties. The smaller the file size, the faster a PDF document will download. The PDF Optimizer allows you to determine how various PDF document components contribute to its overall file size. You can then target those components to optimize the PDF.

Audit space usage of PDF file components

To determine how PDF file components contribute to file size:

1   Open the PDF file you want to optimize.
2   Choose Advanced, PDF Optimizer to open the PDF Optimizer dialog box.
3   Click Audit space usage to open the Audit Space Usage dialog box, shown in Exhibit 3-9.
4   Click OK.

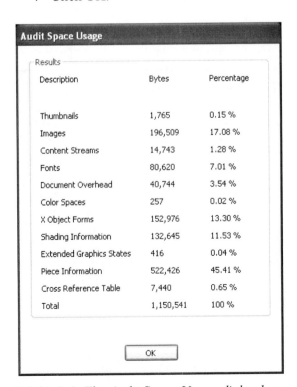

Exhibit 3-9: The Audit Space Usage dialog box

Optimizing a PDF document

To optimize a PDF document:

1 Open the PDF document.

2 Choose Advanced, PDF Optimizer to open the PDF Optimizer dialog box, shown in Exhibit 3-10.

3 From the Settings list, select an optimization preset, if any exist. To create your own preset, specify optimization settings, and then click Save to add the custom settings as a named preset.

4 From the Make compatible with list, select the version of Acrobat you want the optimized file to be compatible with.

5 From the categories on the left, select each category, and specify the optimization settings you want to use.

6 Click OK to optimize the file using the specified settings.

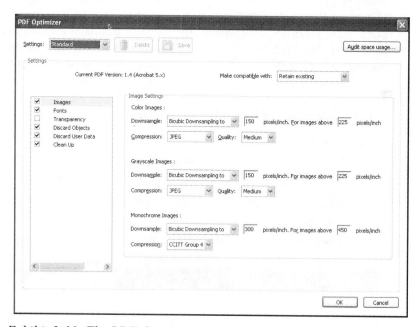

Exhibit 3-10: The PDF Optimizer dialog box

The following table describes the setting categories in the dialog box.

Category	Description
Images	Specify compression options for color, grayscale, and monochrome images.
Fonts	Specify any fonts you want to unembed (remove) to decrease file size. If you unembed fonts, users who do not have the fonts that are in use in the document will view the document with font substitutions instead. If you want to ensure that users will see the document text precisely as designed, don't unembed fonts.
Transparency	Specify settings for flattening transparent areas within artwork to reduce file size.
Discard Objects	Specify objects you want to remove from the document to reduce file size.
Discard User Data	Specify personal information you want to remove from the document.
Clean Up	Specify options for removing elements in the document that you don't need.

D-1: Reducing PDF file size

Here's how	Here's why
1 Open Optimize.pdf	(From the current unit folder.) This file was originally created in Adobe Illustrator. You'll check its file size to determine whether you should optimize some of its content to reduce its file size.
2 Choose **Advanced**, **PDF Optimizer...**	To open the PDF Optimizer dialog box.
Click **Audit space usage**	(In the top-right corner.) To open the Audit Space Usage dialog box. The total file size is more than a million bytes. Illustrator includes data you don't need in the file, so you'll remove it, and also flatten transparency.
Click **OK**	
3 From the Settings list, select **Standard**	(If necessary.) To begin with the standard settings.
4 In the list of categories, check **Transparency**	To make the transparency settings active.
Under Preset, verify that **[Medium Resolution]** is selected	
5 In the list of categories, select **Discard User Data**	Click the category name. Do not clear the category check box.
Check **Discard private data of other applications**	To remove any data that is present only for use with Illustrator.
Click **OK**	To open the Save Optimized As dialog box.
6 In the File name box, enter **My Optimize**	
Click **Save**	To save the optimized file in the current unit folder. You'll verify the results of the optimization settings you applied.
7 Choose **Advanced**, **PDF Optimizer...**	To open the PDF Optimizer dialog box.
Click **Audit space usage**	To open the Audit Space Usage dialog box. The file size is now less than half of its original size.
Click **OK**	

8 Click **OK**	To open the Save Optimized As dialog box.
Click **Cancel**	
9 Close the document	

Unit summary: Modifying PDF documents

Topic A
In this topic, you learned how to use the **Pages panel** to **arrange** pages, **move** pages between documents, **delete** pages, and **extract** pages.

Topic B
In this topic, you learned how to modify document text, add **headers** and **footers**, and modify the **page numbering** in a PDF document.

Topic C
In this topic, you learned that you can move content from a PDF document to files created in other programs. You also learned that you can save a PDF document to several file types, including Encapsulated PostScript (EPS), HTML, JPEG, RTF, Microsoft Word, text, or XML. Finally, you learned how to copy a graphic from a PDF document into another file.

Topic D
In this topic, you learned how to **optimize** a PDF document by using the PDF Optimizer. You learned that optimizing a PDF document **reduces the file size**, which allows it to download faster.

Independent practice activity

In this activity, you'll move pages between PDF documents. You'll also edit PDF text and extract a PDF page. Then you'll add a header and footer, customize page numbering, and copy content from a PDF file. Finally, you'll optimize a PDF document.

1 Open Modifying.pdf from the current unit folder.

2 Save the file as **My Modifying** in the current unit folder.

3 Open Copying.pdf from the current unit folder and tile the two windows vertically.

4 Move the first page of Copying.pdf to the beginning of My Modifying.pdf.

5 Close Copying.pdf and maximize My Modifying.pdf.

6 On page 1, in the text below "From D. Reynolds," change the extension from 301 to **310**. (*Hint*: Use the TouchUp Text tool on the Advanced Editing toolbar.)

7 Extract the first page of My Modifying.pdf without removing it from the file, and save the extracted copy as **Review intro** (in the current unit folder). Close Review intro.

8 Add a header to the top-right corner of each page and set the header to display the text **September Newsletter for review**.

9 Customize Acrobat's page numbering so that it numbers the pages consecutively, beginning with the second page as page 1. (*Hint*: Use the Number Pages command to specify the second through fifth pages as pages 1 through 4, and to specify that the first page uses a numbering style of None.)

10 Copy the entire Spice Tips story from the last page and paste it into a new document in Microsoft Word. Save the copied story in Microsoft Word as **Spice Tips** (in the current unit folder.) Close Spice Tips and close Microsoft Word. (*Hint*: The Spice Tips story has four paragraphs, all at the bottom of the page. Use the Select tool to highlight the article title and the article.)

11 Optimize the My Modifying.pdf document. (In the PDF Optimizer dialog box, from the Settings list, select **Standard**. In the Discard User Data category, check **Discard private data of other applications**. Click **OK**, and save the optimized file to the current unit folder as **My modifying optimized**.

12 Close all files.

Review questions

1 Which is true about using the Document, Insert Pages command?

A It moves all pages from the PDF file you specify into the current PDF file.

B It moves only selected pages from the PDF file you specify into the current PDF file.

C It moves all pages from the current PDF file into the PDF file you specify.

D It moves only selected pages from the current PDF file into the PDF file you specify.

2 Which statements are true about the TouchUp Text tool? (Choose all that apply.)

A You can use it to select and copy text, but not to edit text.

B You can use it to select, insert, delete, and copy text.

C You can use it to edit text, but only if the text is formatted using a font that's installed on your computer.

D You can use it to edit or copy text, but not to delete text.

3 If you want to apply minor text edits to a PDF file, which tool should you use?

A The Hand tool

B The Select tool

C The Text TouchUp tool

D The Article tool

4 How can you add a header to a PDF file?

A Use the Stamp tool to stamp header text to the top of each page.

B Use the Select tool to add the header text to the top of each page.

C Use the Text TouchUp tool to add the header text to the top of each page.

D Choose Document, Add Headers & Footers.

5 How can you reduce a PDF document's file size so that it downloads faster?

A Choose Advanced, Preflight and apply the desired optimization settings.

B Choose Advanced, PDF Optimizer and apply the desired optimization settings.

C Choose File, Organizer and apply the desired optimization settings.

D Choose Advanced, Security Settings and apply the desired optimization settings.

6 In the Pages panel, how can you select multiple non-sequential pages?

   A Hold down Shift and click the pages you want.

   B To the right of each page thumbnail, check each page you want to select.

   C Hold down Ctrl and then click the pages you want.

   D Double-click a thumbnail, specify the pages to select, and click OK.

7 In the Pages panel, how can you rearrange pages?

   A Beneath a page thumbnail, double-click the page number, enter the new page number, and press Enter.

   B Drag a page thumbnail to a new location.

   C Select a page thumbnail and press Ctrl+U or Ctrl+D to move it up or down in the page count.

   D Double-click a page thumbnail, enter a new page number, and click OK.

Unit 4
Document navigation tools

Unit time: 45 minutes

Complete this unit, and you'll know how to:

A Insert, modify, arrange, and format bookmarks.

B Create and format text links.

Topic A: Bookmarks

This topic covers the following ACE exam objective for Acrobat 8.0 Professional.

#	Objective
5.3	Create and modify bookmarks.

Automatically generated bookmarks

Explanation

When you create a PDF document that you or others will read onscreen, you can insert *bookmarks* that provide users with an easy way to navigate directly to specific content. When you create a PDF document from some programs, such as Microsoft Word, you can make specified content in the document automatically generate bookmarks in the resulting PDF document. Some programs don't offer this feature, but you can always create bookmarks directly within Acrobat.

If the source program you're using has an Adobe PDF menu, you can convert documents created in that program to PDF and automatically create bookmarks based on document content. For example, you can make all headings in a Word document bookmarks in the resulting PDF.

Do it!

A-1: Testing automatically generated bookmarks

Here's how	Here's why
1 Open Project.pdf	From the current unit folder.
2 Save the file as **My Project**	In the current unit folder.
3 Click	(The Bookmarks button.) To display the Bookmarks panel. These bookmarks were generated automatically when the PDF file was created from an Adobe InDesign document.
4 Click each bookmark	To test them. Each bookmark navigates to its associated content.

The New Bookmark command

Explanation

Some PDF documents might not have any bookmarks, and even when a PDF document contains automatically generated bookmarks, it might not have all the bookmarks you want. You can use Acrobat's New Bookmark command to create bookmarks.

To create a bookmark by using the New Bookmark command:

1 Display the content you want the new bookmark to navigate to.
2 Set the desired magnification for the content that the bookmark will be displayed.
3 Display the Bookmarks panel.
4 At the top of the Bookmarks panel, click the New bookmark button to create an untitled bookmark. You can also press Ctrl+B.

5 Type a name for the new bookmark (to replace the default name, Untitled) and then press Enter. The new bookmark appears below the bookmark that was previously selected in the Bookmarks panel.

Do it!

A-2: Adding a bookmark

Here's how	Here's why
1 Choose **View**, **Go To**, **First Page**	To navigate to page 1. You'll add a bookmark that shows all of page 1.
2 Click as shown	
	(On the Select & Zoom toolbar.) To display the Magnification menu.
Choose **Fit Page**	You can also press Ctrl+0.
3 Click	(The New bookmark button is at the top of the Bookmarks panel.) To create a new bookmark.
Type **Cover** and press ⏎ ENTER	To name the new bookmark. The bookmark appears below whichever bookmark was selected when you clicked the New bookmark button.
4 Click **Executive Summary**	(In the Bookmarks panel.) To navigate to another bookmark's content.
5 Click **Cover**	To return to the content associated with the Cover bookmark.
6 Navigate to page 2	(The table of contents page.) You'll add another bookmark that navigates to page 2 at Fit Width view.
Display the Magnification menu and choose **Fit Width**	To fit the page width in the window.
7 Create a new bookmark named **Contents**	Click the New bookmark button, enter Contents, and press Enter.
8 Click each of the two new bookmarks	The Cover bookmark displays page 1 at Fit Page view, and the Contents bookmark displays page 2 at Fit Width view.

Bookmarks from selected text

Explanation

When you're creating a bookmark that will navigate to specific text, such as a heading, you can generate the bookmark quickly by using the Select tool. This technique allows you to add a bookmark that's automatically named based on the selected text.

To generate a bookmark from selected text:

1   Navigate to the content and magnification that you want the bookmark to display.

2   In the Select & Zoom toolbar, select the Select tool.

3   Select the text on which you want to base the bookmark.

4   Right-click the selected text and choose Add Bookmark. The new bookmark appears in the Bookmarks panel, with a name based on the selected text.

Do it!

A-3:   Adding bookmarks from selected text

Here's how	Here's why
1 Click **The Project Team**	(In the Bookmarks panel.) To view the Project Team story. This story contains two subheadings, "Employees" and "Consultants." You'll create bookmarks for these items.
Scroll down so the Employees subheading is at the top of the window	
Specify Fit Width magnification	If necessary.
Verify that the Select tool is active	In the Select & Zoom toolbar.
2 Select the **Employees** subheading	*Employees* Ann Salinski, VP Financial Ann's role is to oversee th
3 Right-click the selected text	
Choose **Add Bookmark**	To add the selected text as a bookmark whose destination is based on the current view and whose name matches the selected text. The new bookmark appears below the most recently selected bookmark, which in this case was "The Project Team."
4 Scroll down so the Consultants subheading is at the top of the window	
5 Create a bookmark for the Consultants subheading	Use the Select tool to select the subheading. Right-click the selected text and choose Add Bookmark from the shortcut menu.
6 Click	To select the Hand tool.
Click anywhere on the page	To deselect the subheading text.
7 Test the new bookmarks	
8 Save the document	

Modifying bookmark destinations

Explanation

When you create a PDF document with automatically generated bookmarks, the resulting bookmarks might not function as you intend. For example, the bookmarks might navigate to the content you want, but not the desired magnification.

To modify a bookmark destination:

1 Navigate to the desired content and magnification.
2 In the Bookmarks panel, right-click the bookmark. From the shortcut menu, choose Set Destination. A warning dialog box appears, asking you to verify that you want to change the bookmark's destination.
3 Click Yes.

Bookmark actions

Each bookmark has an *action* that determines what happens when you click the bookmark. A bookmark can perform actions other than navigating to a destination. For example, you can set a bookmark to execute a menu command or open a file. You can view a bookmark's properties to determine its current action and apply a different action if necessary.

To view and modify a bookmark's action:

1 Right-click the bookmark and choose Properties to open the Bookmark Properties dialog box.
2 Activate the Actions tab. The bookmark's current action is listed in the Actions list, as shown in Exhibit 4-1.
3 Specify any changes to the bookmark's action and click Close.

   • Select the action and click Delete to remove it.
   • Select the action and click Edit to change it.
   • To add a new action, select an action from the Select Action list and click Add.

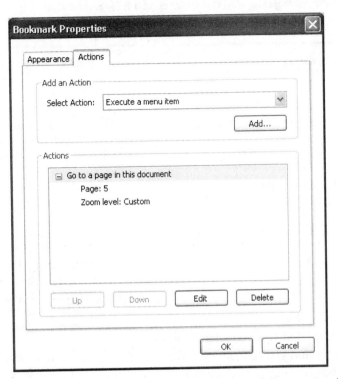

Exhibit 4-1: The Actions tab in the Bookmark Properties dialog box

A-4: Modifying bookmark destinations

Here's how	Here's why
1 Click **Cover**	(In the Bookmarks panel.) To view the Cover page. You created this bookmark to be displayed at Fit Page view.
2 Click **Executive Summary**	(In the Bookmarks panel.) To view the Executive Summary section. This bookmark also appears at Fit Page view.
3 Click **Contents**	(In the Bookmarks panel.) You created this bookmark to display at Fit Width view.
4 Click **Executive Summary**	When you clicked this bookmark earlier, it displayed its associated page at Fit Page view. Now it displays the page at Fit Width view. The automatically generated bookmarks navigate to a specific page but don't specify a particular magnification. You'll modify these bookmarks to always use Fit Width magnification.
5 Verify that you're viewing the Executive Summary page at Fit Width view	You'll modify the bookmark's destination based on the current view in the document pane.
6 Right-click the **Executive Summary** bookmark	
Choose **Set Destination**	(From the shortcut menu.) To change this bookmark's destination to use the view currently displayed in the document pane.
Click **Yes**	To set the new destination.
7 Click **Cover**, and then click **Executive Summary**	To verify that the Executive Summary bookmark uses Fit Width magnification, regardless of the document's magnification before you click the bookmark.
8 Click **The Project Team**	(The next automatically generated bookmark.) Because this bookmark is set to retain the current magnification, it uses Fit Width. However, if another magnification had been in use, then it would continue using that magnification. You'll set it to always use Fit Width magnification.
9 Set the current view as this bookmark's destination	Right-click the bookmark and choose Set Destination; then click Yes.

10 Set the remaining bookmarks to use Fit Width magnification	(The Project Justification, Progress Update, and Outstanding Issues for Phase One bookmarks.) Click each bookmark to navigate to its current destination; then right-click the bookmark and choose Set Destination.
11 Save the document	

Organizing bookmarks

Explanation

When you're finished adding bookmarks, you might want to rearrange the order of the bookmarks in the Bookmarks panel. To move a bookmark, drag it to a desired position in the list of bookmarks. A horizontal line appears next to the pointer as you drag, indicating the position you're moving the bookmark to.

If some bookmarks represent major document sections while others represent minor or secondary content sections, you might want to nest the secondary bookmarks below an appropriate major bookmark. A *nested* bookmark is one that falls under a broader category of its parent bookmark.

For example, if you have one bookmark named "Recipes," and you have several recipe bookmarks, it would make sense to nest the individual recipe bookmarks under the broader category that is the "Recipes" bookmark. Nested bookmarks appear indented below their parent bookmark. To nest bookmarks, select the bookmarks you want to nest and drag them below and to the right of the parent bookmark. The horizontal line that appears next to the pointer will indent to the right when it's in the correct position.

Do it!

A-5: Arranging bookmarks

Here's how	Here's why
1 Observe the bookmarks	(In the Bookmarks panel.) The Cover bookmark should be first and the Contents bookmark should be second. The Employees and Consultants bookmarks should be nested below the "The Project Team" bookmark to indicate that they're subheadings.
2 Drag **Cover** upward until a line appears above the first bookmark, as shown	The Cover bookmark is now first in the list.
3 Move the **Contents** bookmark below the Cover bookmark	

4 Click **Employees**	To select it.
Hold down (CTRL) and click **Consultants**	

```
📄 The Project Team
📄 Employees
📄 Consultants
📄 Project Justification
```

To select both bookmarks.

Release (CTRL)	
5 Drag the selected bookmarks up and to the right, as shown	

```
📄 The Project Team
📄 Employees
📄 Consultants
📄 Project Justification
```

Drag until an indented line appears below "The Project Team."

6 Observe the bookmarks	

```
□ 📄 The Project Team
      📄 Employees
      📄 Consultants
```

The subheading bookmarks are nested below the "The Project Team" bookmark.

7 Click ⊟	(Next to "The Project Team.") To collapse the bookmark, hiding the nested bookmarks.
8 Expand the bookmark	(Click the + button next to the bookmark name.) To show the nested bookmarks.
9 Save the document	

Bookmark formatting

Explanation

When a PDF document includes many bookmarks that you can categorize into groups, you might want to format groups of bookmarks so that each group appears distinct from the other groups. You can format bookmarks to appear in bold, italic, or bold-italic text. You can also apply a color to bookmarks.

To format bookmarks:

1 Select the bookmarks you want to format.

2 At the top of the Bookmarks panel, from the Options menu, choose Properties.

3 In the Properties dialog box, activate the Appearance tab.

4 From the Style list, select the desired style.

5 From the Color list, select the desired color.

6 Click OK.

Wrapping long bookmark names

If a bookmark name is too long to fit in the Bookmarks panel, it appears cut off. You can force long bookmark names to wrap inside the panel so the entire name is always visible. To wrap bookmark names, from the Bookmarks panel's Options menu, choose Wrap Long Bookmarks.

Do it!

A-6:   Formatting bookmarks

Here's how	Here's why
1 Click the first bookmark	You'll apply bold formatting to all the top-level bookmarks.
Hold down ⬭SHIFT⬭ and click the last bookmark	To select all bookmarks from the first to the last. The nested bookmarks are not selected.
2 In the Bookmarks panel, choose **Options**, **Properties...**	To open the Bookmark Properties dialog box.
Verify that the Appearance tab is activated	
3 From the Style list, select **Bold**	
Click the color box	A palette appears.
Select the dark red color	(The color square below the black square.) The bookmarks will appear in this color.
Click **OK**	To apply the formatting to the selected bookmarks.
4 Click a blank area in the Bookmarks pane	To deselect the other bookmarks so you can see the formatting.
5 In the Bookmarks panel, click **Options** and verify that Wrap Long Bookmarks is checked	To ensure that long bookmarks will wrap as necessary so their full names are always visible in the Bookmarks panel.
6 Save the document	

Topic B: Working with links

Creating links

Explanation

To use a bookmark, you need to open the Bookmarks panel. However, you can add links that users can click within the PDF document itself, similar to the links on a Web page. You can add links anywhere in a PDF document by using the Link tool, or you can create links based on text you select using the Select tool. When a user clicks a link, it navigates directly to the linked content.

The Link tool

You can use the Link tool to add a link to any part of a PDF document. The link you create will appear in the shape of a rectangle, and you can set its borders to be visible or invisible.

To create a link:

1 Choose Tools, Advanced Editing, Link Tool. (You can also click the Link tool on the Advanced Editing toolbar.)

2 On a page, drag to create a link rectangle. When you release the mouse button, the Create Link dialog box appears, as shown in Exhibit 4-2.

3 Under Link Appearance, from the Link Type list, select an option to specify whether the link rectangle's border will be visible or invisible.

4 Under Link Action, select Go to a page view and click Next to open the Create Go to View dialog box.

5 Navigate to the content and magnification to which you want the link to navigate, and then click Set Link.

6 If you later want to adjust a link's appearance or action, double-click the link by using the Link tool to open the Link Properties dialog box, specify the new settings, and click Close.

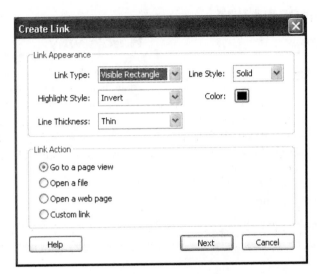

Exhibit 4-2: The Create Link dialog box

If you don't want your links to appear with a rectangle around them, choose an invisible option from the Link Type list. If the link borders are set to invisible, they will be visible only when the Link tool or Select Object tool is selected. If you specify a visible border, you can customize its appearance by selecting an option from the Line Style list, and by selecting a rectangle color from the Color list.

B-1:   Creating a link

Here's how	Here's why
1 Click **Contents**	(In the Bookmarks panel.) To display the contents list. You'll create a link for each item in the contents list.
2 Choose **Tools**, **Advanced Editing**, **Link Tool**	To select the Link tool.
3 Drag to create a rectangular link around the first item, as shown	

	The Create Link dialog box appears.
4 From the Link Type list, select **Invisible Rectangle**	(If necessary.) The rectangle's border will be invisible on the page, and will be visible only when the Link tool or Select Object tool is selected.
5 Under Link Action, select **Go to a page view**	If necessary.
Click **Next**	The Create Go to View dialog box appears. You'll navigate to the view that you want to display when someone clicks the link. The easiest way to navigate to the view you want in this case is to click a bookmark.
In the Bookmarks panel, click **Executive Summary**	To go to the view specified by the bookmark.
Click **Set Link**	
	(In the Create Go to View dialog box.) To complete the link and return to the contents list.

6 Click [hand icon]	On the Select & Zoom toolbar.
Point to the link	*Executive Summary* [pointing finger cursor]
	The pointer changes to a pointing finger, indicating that it's a link. You can click anywhere inside the rectangle you drew to activate the link.
Click the link	To test it.
7 Go back to the previous view	On the Page Navigation toolbar, click the left-pointing arrow button.
8 Create additional links for the remaining contents items	(Use the Link tool to drag around each item. In the Create Link dialog box, click Next. Navigate to the appropriate destination and click Set Link.) In the next activity, you'll resize the link rectangles.

Setting links to align and match size

Explanation

If you're creating multiple links on one page, you might want to ensure that the links use the same height and width to ensure consistency and make the links easy to use. You can also align links to one another.

To set multiple links to the same size:

1 Select the Link tool or the Select Object tool.

2 Click a link to select it; then hold down the Ctrl key and click each additional link that you want to select.

3 Right-click the selected link whose size you want the other links to match, and select an option from the Size submenu. The link you right-click becomes the *anchor* object. You can force the other links to match the anchor object's height and width.

To select multiple continuous links, you can click the first link, hold the Shift key, and click the last link in the sequence to select the entire range of links. The last link you select appears with a red border, and the other links appear with blue borders. The object with a red border is the anchor object, and it remains unchanged while the other items adjust to match it.

You can also align selected links by right-clicking one of them and selecting an option from the Align submenu.

Do it!

B-2: Resizing and aligning links

Here's how	Here's why
1 Select the Link tool	(Choose Tools, Advanced Editing, Link Tool.) You'll select all the links so you can size them to match.
2 Click the first link	To select it.
Hold down (SHIFT) and click the last link	To select all the links in the list. The last link appears with a red border, indicating that by default, it's the anchor object whose size the other objects will match.
3 Right-click a link of your choice	You'll set this link as the anchor object.
Select **Size**, **Both**	(From the shortcut menu.) To size all links to match the anchor object's height and width. The link sizes are now all equal, but they might not align to one another.
4 Right-click a link of your choice	
From the shortcut menu, select **Align**, **Left**	To align the links to the left edge of the anchor object.
5 Save the document	

Modifying text color

Explanation

If a text link does not appear differently than ordinary text, users won't know that it's a link. Many text links on Web pages appear as blue underlined text. You can format text links within a PDF document to use this formatting (or other colors) as a cue to readers that a section of text is a link. You can use the Link Properties dialog box to specify a blue underline for a text link, but this won't apply the blue color to the text itself. You can format the text color by using the TouchUp Text tool.

To format the color of text in a PDF document:

1. Choose Tools, Advanced Editing, TouchUp Text tool. (You can also click the TouchUp Text tool on the Advanced Editing toolbar.)
2. Select the text you want to format.
3. Right-click the selected text and choose Properties to open the TouchUp Properties dialog box.
4. Activate the Text tab.
5. Click the Fill list and select the desired color.
6. Click Close.

Do it!

B-3: Formatting text to look like a link

Here's how	Here's why
1 Click **Executive Summary**	(In the Bookmarks panel.) You'll create a link based on text in the summary. Before you create the link, you'll make the text blue so it looks like a standard Web link.
2 Select the TouchUp Text tool	Choose Tools, Advanced Editing, TouchUp Text Tool, or click the TouchUp Text tool in the Advanced Editing toolbar.
3 In the second paragraph's first sentence, select **project team**	
4 Right-click the selected text	
Choose **Properties...**	To open the TouchUp Properties dialog box. A TouchUp warning message might appear, indicating that the original font is not available. If so, a substituted font will be used.
Click **OK**	If necessary.
5 Next to Fill, click the black swatch	A color palette appears.
Select the bright blue color	You'll make the text appear as a standard Web link.
Click **Close**	To apply the blue color.
6 Click anywhere on the page	To deselect the link to view the new text color.

Text links

Explanation

After you've formatted the text that you want to serve as a link, you need to use the Select tool to create the link. To create a text link:

1 On the Select & Zoom toolbar, select the Select tool.

2 Select the text that you want to serve as a link.

3 Right-click the selected text and choose Create Link to open the Create Link dialog box, shown in Exhibit 4-3.

4 If you want the text link to display a blue underline, select Visible Rectangle from the Link Type list. From the Line Style list, select Underline. From the Fill list, select a color.

5 Under Link Action, select Go to a page view.

6 Click Next to open the Create Go to a View dialog box.

7 Navigate to the destination you want the link to navigate to and click Set Link.

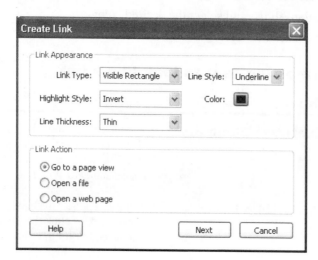

Exhibit 4-3: The Create Link dialog box

Do it!   **B-4:   Creating links from selected text**

Here's how	Here's why
1 Select the Select tool	
2 Select the blue text	The "project team" text.
Right-click the selected text	
Choose **Create Link**	(From the shortcut menu.) To open the Create Link dialog box.
3 From the Link Type list, select **Visible Rectangle**	You'll set this link to show an underline to help readers identify it as a link.
From the Line Style list, select **Underline**	Underlined links are a standard user interface convention on the Web. You'll format this link according to that standard style.
Set the underline's color to blue	Next to Fill, click the black swatch and select the bright blue color.
4 Under Link Action, select **Go to a page view**	If necessary.
5 Click **Next**	To open the Create Go to View dialog box.
In the Bookmarks panel, click **The Project Team**	To navigate to the view you want to use for the link.
Click **Set Link**	In the Create Go to View dialog box.
6 Click 🖐	You'll test the link.
7 Click anywhere on the page	*w of the project team members, progress on this initiative, and*
	To deselect the link text. The link appears blue with a blue underline.
8 Point to the link	The pointer changes to a pointing finger, indicating that it's a link.
9 Click the link	To test it.
10 Save and close the document	

Unit summary: Document navigation tools

Topic A

In this topic, you learned how to create **bookmarks** and modify bookmark destinations. You also learned how to **arrange** and **nest** bookmarks in the Bookmarks panel. Finally, you learned how to **format bookmarks**.

Topic B

In this topic, you learned how to create **links** using the Link tool. You **resized** and **aligned** links to the **anchor object**, and you created a text link from selected text and formatted it so that users will know that it's a link.

Independent practice activity

In this activity, you'll create and modify bookmarks. You'll create and format a text link.

1 Open Navigation.pdf from the current unit folder.

2 Save the file as **My Navigation** in the current unit folder.

3 Modify the destinations for the automatically generated bookmarks to display their respective content at Fit Width magnification.

4 Create a bookmark for page 1 named **Cover** that displays the page at Fit Page magnification.

5 Move the Cover bookmark to the top of the bookmarks list.

6 In the Spices of the Month story, create a bookmark that displays the Bay Leaves subheading at Fit Width magnification. Create a second bookmark that displays the Cilantro/Coriander subheading at Fit Width magnification.

7 Nest the Bay Leaves and Cilantro/Coriander bookmarks below the Spices of the Month bookmark.

8 Create an invisible link for each item on the table of contents on page 1 by using the Link tool. Size and align the links to match each other.

9 On page 1 in the second paragraph's second line, format the text "helpful recipes" as blue text. (*Hint*: Use the TouchUp Text tool.)

10 Add a link to the blue text that displays a blue underline and navigates to the "Outlander Cooking" story on page two, at Fit Width magnification. (*Hint*: Select the text by using the Select tool, right-click the selected text, and choose **Create Link**.)

11 Save and close the document.

Review questions

1 Which statements are true about bookmarks? (Choose all that apply.)

   A You can generate bookmarks automatically from some source programs when you generate a PDF file.

   B Bookmarks are stored in the Bookmarks panel, and don't appear directly in the document text.

   C You can create a bookmark by dragging the Bookmark tool across an item.

   D You can create a bookmark by navigating to the content you want the bookmark to display, and then clicking the New bookmark button in the Bookmarks panel.

2 Which of the following are ways to create bookmarks? (Choose all that apply.)

   A Select some text, right-click the text, and choose Add Bookmark.

   B Select some text and Ctrl-click anywhere on the selected text.

   C Navigate to a page in the document and click the New bookmark button in the Bookmarks panel.

   D Navigate to a page in the document and press Ctrl+B.

3 You want to allow users to navigate a PDF document by using Web-like text links. Which tool should you use?

   A The Bookmark tool

   B The Article tool

   C The Link tool

   D The Crop tool

4 Why is it important to format text links?

5 How can you create a link?

   A Select the Link tool and drag to create a rectangle around the content you want to use for the link trigger.

   B Use the TouchUp Text tool to select the content you want to use for the link trigger, right-click the content, and choose Create Link.

   C Select the content you want to use for the link trigger and choose Document, Create Link.

   D Select the Link tool and Ctrl-click the content you want to use for the link trigger.

Unit 5

PDF accessibility

Unit time: 45 minutes

Complete this unit, and you'll know how to:

A Optimize the accessibility of the PDF documents that you distribute.

B Modify the Acrobat environment to help you access PDF content.

Topic A: Accessible documents

Enhancing document accessibility

Explanation

You can use Acrobat 8.0 Professional to create PDF documents that are accessible to people with disabilities such as vision or mobility impairments. Accessible PDF documents provide content that's presented coherently when accessed via assistive technologies such as screen readers, or when accessed via the accessibility features built into Acrobat or Adobe Reader.

Users with disabilities can access PDF content with specialized software and devices, such as a screen magnifier or screen reader, or by using the accessibility options in Acrobat and Acrobat Reader. A screen magnifier is an application that displays onscreen content at an increased magnification to help people with poor vision. A screen reader is an application that identifies the content displayed onscreen and reads it aloud, or converts it to Braille characters on a Braille display.

Accessibility tags

When users open a document, they can determine the document's structure based on text formatting (such as headings and subheadings) and other cues that help them read the content in the intended sequence. However, assistive technologies, such as screen reader software, typically cannot interpret purely visual content structures, and therefore might present content in the wrong sequence. You can add tags to a document that specify the document's structure so that screen readers and other assistive technologies can interpret and present the content as intended.

For best results, you should generate tags when the document is initially converted to PDF from its authoring application. For example, if you're converting a Microsoft Word document to PDF by using PDFMaker, you should check Enable accessibility and reflow with Tagged PDF (which is checked by default) on the Settings tab of the Acrobat PDFMaker dialog box. PDFMaker then generates a PDF document that has tags based on the document's content. You can also use Acrobat 8.0 Professional to add tags to an untagged PDF document, or modify the tags of an already tagged document.

Accessibility tags also help make your PDF content easier to view on handheld devices such as cell phones. For example, tagged PDF documents will reflow on the smaller screens of handheld devices.

Determining if a PDF document is tagged

If you don't know if an existing PDF document is tagged or not, you can check its tag status by using the Document Properties dialog box. To determine if a PDF document is tagged:

1 Choose File, Properties to open the Document Properties dialog box.
2 Activate the Description tab.
3 Under Advanced, observe the Tagged PDF item. Either Yes or No appears next to this item to indicate if the document is tagged.

Viewing the tag tree

Tags don't affect a document's appearance. If you want to view the tags in a document, you can view the *tag tree*. Each item in the tag tree represents an item in the document, such as a heading, a paragraph, or a graphic. To display a document's tag tree, choose View, Navigation Panels, Tags. The tag tree lists tags hierarchically, to reflect their reading sequence. Each tag is coded by an element type that appears within < > characters, and identifies the type of content. Initially, the Tags panel displays only a single item, called the Tags root. You can expand the Tags root to display the next level of tags. To expand all tags at once, as shown in Exhibit 5-1, press Ctrl when you expand the Tags root.

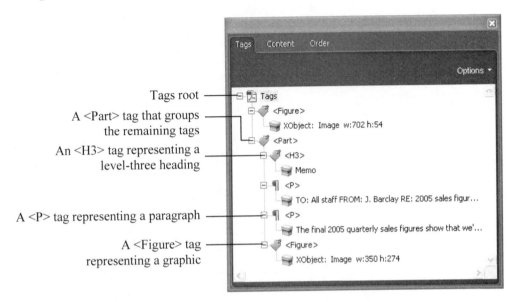

Tags root

A <Part> tag that groups the remaining tags

An <H3> tag representing a level-three heading

A <P> tag representing a paragraph

A <Figure> tag representing a graphic

Exhibit 5-1: The tags tree in the Tags panel

Inserting tags in a PDF document

To insert tags, choose Advanced, Accessibility, Add Tags To Document. You can also add tags from the Tags panel's Options menu by choosing Add Tags to Document.

A-1: Adding tags to a PDF document

Here's how	Here's why
1 Open Add tags.pdf	From the current unit folder.
Save the file as **My Add tags**	You'll determine if this is a tagged file.
2 Choose **File**, **Properties...**	To open the Document Properties dialog box.
Activate the Description tab	If necessary.
3 Observe the Tagged PDF item	

```
┌─Advanced──────────────────────────┐
│  PDF Producer:  Acrobat Distiller 7.0 ( │
│   PDF Version:  1.4 (Acrobat 5.x)       │
│     Location:   C:\Student Data\Unit│
│     File Size:  16.40 KB (16,794 Byt│
│    Page Size:   8.50 x 11.00 in         │
│   Tagged PDF:   No                      │
└───────────────────────────────────┘
```

(Under Advanced.) The word No appears, indicating that this document is not tagged.

Click **OK**	To close the dialog box. You'll add tags from within the Tags panel so that you can see the tags as you insert them.
4 Choose **View**, **Navigation Panels**, **Tags**	

```
┌────────────────────────────────────┐
│ Tags    Content    Order            │
│                                     │
│                                     │
│   📄 No Tags available              │
│                                     │
└────────────────────────────────────┘
```

To open the Tags panel.

5 From the Options menu, choose **Add Tags to Document**	

```
┌────────────────────────────────────┐
│ Tags    Content    Order            │
│                                     │
│                                     │
│  ⊞ 📄 Tags                          │
│                                     │
└────────────────────────────────────┘
```

A single item appears in the Tags panel. You can expand it to display its contents.

6 Next to the Tags root, click **+**

To expand the Tags root. Several tags appear, but you'll have to expand them to display their contents.

Next to the Tags root, click **−**

To collapse the Tags root. You'll expand all the items in the Tags root at once.

Press ⬭CTRL⬭ and click **+**

To expand all the contents at once.

7 Drag the Tags tab below the Navigation panel buttons

To add a button for the Tags panel to the Navigation panel so that you can activate it more quickly the next time you need it.

Close the floating panel that you dragged the Tags tab from

To clear up more space on the screen.

8 Save the document

Checking accessibility

Explanation

When you use Acrobat 8.0 Professional to add tags to a PDF document, the Navigation panel displays a report listing potential problems with the document tags, as shown in Exhibit 5-2. You can click the links in the report to navigate to the problem areas, and follow the instructions to fix any problems.

Exhibit 5-2: The Recognition Report in the Navigation panel

Full accessibility check

You can't save or print the report that's generated when you add tags to a document, and the report appears only when you add tags from within Acrobat. To generate a detailed report at any time, which includes tips for fixing problems, perform a full accessibility check. To do so:

1 Choose Advanced, Accessibility, Full Check to open the Accessibility Full Check dialog box, shown in Exhibit 5-3.

2 Specify the options you want to use, and then click Start Checking to generate the report. A dialog box will appear, summarizing any problems that might exist.

3 Click OK to close the dialog box. The Accessibility Report appears in the Navigation panel.

4 Read through the Accessibility Report and fix any listed problems.

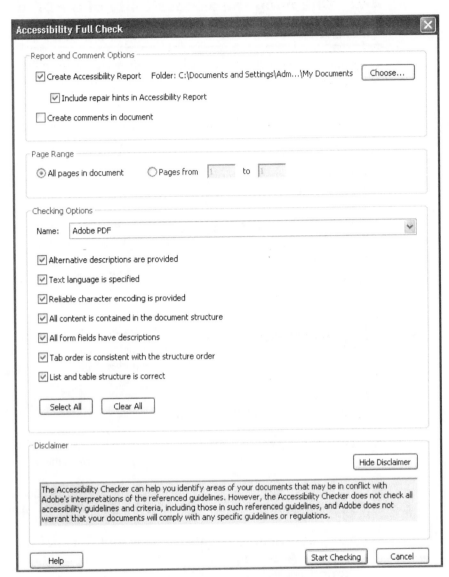

Exhibit 5-3: The Accessibility Full Check dialog box

Quick accessibility check

If you want to perform a quick check to ensure that the document has the minimum attributes necessary for basic accessibility, then choose Advanced, Accessibility, Quick Check. A dialog box will appear displaying a summary of any problems. Click OK to close the dialog box.

Do it!

A-2: Checking the accessibility of a PDF document

Here's how	Here's why
1 Activate the Recognition Report panel	(Click the Recognition Report button.) This report was automatically generated when you added tags to this document.
2 In the Recognition Report panel, click **Introduction**	To navigate to a description of the report and how you can use it.
3 Scroll down in the Recognition Report panel	
Click **Back to the Top**	To return to the top of the report in the Navigation panel.
4 Read the text under Accessibility	The document includes two graphics with no alternate text, which is helpful to users with assistive devices such a screen readers.
5 Close the Recognition Report panel	You'll generate a more complete report that includes basic instructions for fixing potential problems.
6 Choose **Advanced**, **Accessibility**, **Full Check...**	To open the Accessibility Full Check dialog box.
Click **Choose...**	(At the top of the dialog box.) To open the Browse For Folder dialog box.
Navigate to the current unit folder and click **OK**	To specify the location where you want to save the HTML file containing the report data.
7 Verify that **Include repair hints in Accessibility Report** is checked	Under Report and Comment Options.
Verify that all the items under Checking Options are checked	
Click **Start Checking**	A dialog box appears, indicating that two figures have no alternate text, and that a language isn't specified for the document.
Click **OK**	The Accessibility Report appears in the Navigation panel. In addition, an HTML version of the report is saved in the folder you specified.
8 Observe the report	(In the Navigation panel.) The report includes a link to hints that you can click to view instructions for fixing the accessibility problems.

Fixing potential accessibility problems

Explanation

If you performed a full check to reveal accessibility problems, you can follow the instructions in the Accessibility Report displayed in the Navigation panel.

Specifying the language in use in a document

Specifying the language in use in a PDF document ensures that the correct dictionary is used to check the document's spelling. It also helps users with assistive devices to understand what they're working with. To specify a language for a PDF document:

1 Choose File, Properties to open the Document Properties dialog box.
2 Activate the Advanced tab.
3 Under Reading Options, from the Language list, select the language you want to associate with the document.
4 Click OK.

If some items in your document use a language other than the language specified for the entire document, you can specify a language for individual tags. For example, if you have a document written in English that also contains specific words or phrases in Latin, you can tag those terms appropriately. To specify the language for a tagged item:

1 In the Tags panel, select the tag whose language you want to specify individually.
2 From the Tags panel's Options menu, select Properties to open the TouchUp Properties dialog box.
3 Activate the Tag tab, if necessary.
4 From the Language list, select a language.
5 Click Close.

The language you specify will be associated with the tag you selected, as well as any tags subordinate to it in the tag tree.

Specifying alternate text for graphics

Screen readers ignore graphics in a document because graphics are visual and therefore meaningless to those who use screen readers and other assistive devices. If a graphic contains text or other information that you want all users to access, then you should include alternate text. For example, if you have a corporate logo that reads XYZ Corporation, your alternate text should read "XYZ Corporation." Or, if you have an image of your company's CEO, your alternate text should indicate his or her name and title. You can do this within the authoring application you used to create the original document, or you can specify alternate text from within Acrobat.

To specify alternate text for a graphic:

1 In the Tags panel, select the Figure tag for the image.
2 From the Tags panel's Options menu, select Properties to open the TouchUp Properties dialog box.
3 Activate the Tag tab, if necessary.
4 In the Alternate Text box, enter the alternate text for the image.
5 Click Close.

A-3: Fixing accessibility problems

Here's how	Here's why
1 Choose **File**, **Properties...**	You'll specify English as the language for the entire document.
Activate the Advanced tab	
From the Language list, select **English US**	
Click **OK**	
2 In the Navigation panel, click the **Tags** button	To activate the Tags panel. You'll use the Tags panel to add alternate text to the two figures. First, you'll set a highlight to appear on each tagged item when you select its tag in the tag tree.
3 From the Options menu, choose **Highlight Content**	
Expand all the tags	(If necessary.) Hold down Ctrl and click the plus sign next to Tags.
4 In the tag tree, click the first **<Figure>** tag, as shown	
	An outline appears around the logo graphic at the top of the document, to help you associate the tag with its corresponding item in the PDF.
5 From the Options menu, choose **Properties...**	To open the TouchUp Properties dialog box.
Verify that the Tag tab is selected	
In the Alternate Text box, enter **Outlander Spices: Adding spice to your life**	So that the alternate text for this image matches the text in the image that can't be read by screen readers. Screen readers will ignore the image and read this text instead.
Click **Close**	

6 Click the second **<Figure>** tag

(Near the bottom of the tag tree.) This is the tag for the chart graphic.

From the Options menu, choose **Properties...**

To open the TouchUp Properties dialog box.

In the Alternate Text box, enter the text as shown

Alternate Text:	First quarter sales: $227,000 Second quarter sales: $245,000 Third quarter sales: $225,000 Fourth quarter sales: $275,000

Click **Close**

7 Save and close the document

Modifying the reading order

Explanation
To ensure that a screen reader reads a document's content in the intended sequence, you can view and modify the document's *reading order*, which is also called the *page content order*. To view the reading order, choose Tools, Advanced Editing, TouchUp Reading Order Tool. When you select the TouchUp Reading Order tool, each section of content is covered by a highlighted region, as shown in Exhibit 5-4. Each region is numbered, specifying the order in which a screen reader will read the content. If the automatically generated sequence is not correct, you can change it to ensure that users with screen readers can access your content in the intended sequence.

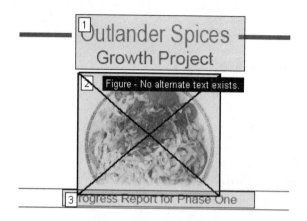

Exhibit 5-4: Highlighted regions showing the reading order for a PDF document

To modify the document reading order:

1 Choose Tools, Advanced Editing, TouchUp Reading Order Tool. The TouchUp Reading Order dialog box appears. If necessary, check Show page content order.

2 In the TouchUp Reading Order dialog box, click Show Order Panel to open the Order panel.

3 In the Order panel, point to the icon next to an item you want to reorder, and drag it up or down to change its position in the reading order.

You also might want to remove an item from the reading order. For example, if you don't plan to add any alternate text to a graphic that's tagged as a figure, you should remove the graphic from the reading order to keep the reading uncluttered. To remove an item from the reading order, in the Order panel, select the item, and from the Options menu, choose Tag as background.

Do it!

A-4: Modifying a tagged document's reading order

Here's how	Here's why
1 Open Reading order.pdf	From the current unit folder.
Save the file as **My Reading order**	
2 Choose **Tools, Advanced Editing, TouchUp Reading Order Tool**	The TouchUp Reading Order dialog box appears.

3　Verify that **Show Page Content Order** is checked

To display highlighted regions for each section of content. You don't need to include the figure in the reading order, because it's a purely visual design component and doesn't convey any important information. You'll use the Order panel to alter the reading order.

4　Click **Show Order Panel**

(In the TouchUp Reading Order dialog box.) To open the Order panel.

5　In the Order panel, under Page 1, click the second item

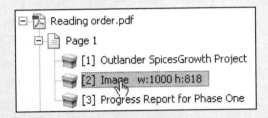

(Representing the highlight region over the image.) The region over the image is selected.

6　Click **Options** and choose **Tag as background**

(In the Order panel.) To remove the image from the reading order. The highlight region over the image disappears, leaving two items in the reading order for this page.

7　Close the TouchUp Reading Order dialog box

Click Close.

Observe the reading order on the page

The reading order is now correct.

8　Save and close the document

Modifying the tag structure

Explanation

If an existing tag structure isn't quite what you need it to be, you might want to remove it altogether and start from scratch, manually tagging document elements to create the tag structure you're looking for.

To create a new tag structure:

1 Select the TouchUp Reading Order tool.

2 In the TouchUp Reading Order dialog box, click Clear Page Structure, and then click Yes.

3 Select the content you want to tag. Use these techniques to add to or subtract from your selection.

- You can add more content to a selection by pressing Shift and dragging over the additional content.

- You can remove content from a selection by pressing Ctrl and dragging over the content you want to remove.

4 In the TouchUp Reading Order dialog box, shown in Exhibit 5-5, click the tag type you want to use for the selected content. A numbered, highlighted region appears over the content you selected.

At any time, you can change the tag type for an existing highlighted region. To do so, select a highlighted region, and in the TouchUp Reading Order dialog box, click the button for the tag type you want to use for the item.

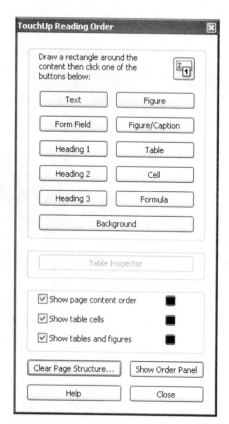

Exhibit 5-5: The TouchUp Reading Order dialog box

Do it!

A-5: Creating a new tagging structure

Here's how	Here's why
1 Open Adjust content.pdf	From the current unit folder.
Save the file as **My Adjust content**	
2 Open the TouchUp Reading Order dialog box	Choose Advanced, Accessibility, TouchUp Reading Order.
Click **Clear Page Structure**	An alert dialog box appears, asking you to verify that you want to delete the page structure.
Click **Yes**	The page structure is removed from the entire document. You'll rebuild the structure for the first page.
3 Double-click the Outlander Spices logo	(At the top of the page.) To select it.
In the TouchUp Reading Order dialog box, click **Figure**	To tag the logo as a figure. This content is marked as the first item in the reading order. You would need to add alternate text to this item before distributing it.
4 Drag across the table of contents, as shown	
In the TouchUp Reading Order dialog box, click **Figure**	This item is marked as the second item in the reading order.

5 Drag across all the text in the left column, as shown

In the TouchUp Reading Order dialog box, click **Text**

6 Drag across the lower text in the right column

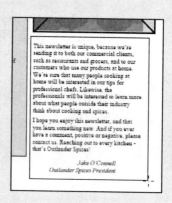

In the TouchUp Reading Order dialog box, click **Text**

This item is marked as the fourth item in the reading order. The new tag structure is more logical than the original structure.

7 Close the TouchUp Reading Order dialog box

8 Save and close the file

Topic B: Accessibility in the Acrobat environment

Accessibility features

Explanation

You can customize the Acrobat environment to help you access PDF content. For example, you can set preferences that enhance Acrobat's ability to work with an assistive device. You can also modify the Acrobat environment to make it more accessible.

The Accessibility Setup Assistant

If you use an assistive device, such as a screen reader or screen magnifier, you can use Acrobat's Accessibility Setup Assistant to choose the preferences that will work best for your device.

To use the Accessibility Setup Assistant to specify accessibility preferences:

1   Choose Advanced, Accessibility, Setup Assistant.
2   Specify the category of settings you want to apply.

- Select Set options for screen readers if you use a device that reads text aloud or generates Braille.
- Select Set options for screen magnifiers if you use a device that displays text at a larger size onscreen.
- Select Set all accessibility options if you use a combination of devices.
- Click Use recommended settings and skip setup to use the recommended settings.

3   Click Next to display the first group of settings you can specify. Continue specifying settings and clicking Next until you're finished.
4   Click Done.

B-1: Using the Accessibility Setup Assistant

Here's how	Here's why
1 Choose **Advanced**, **Accessibility**, **Setup Assistant...**	To open the Accessibility Setup Assistant.
2 Verify that **Set all accessibility options** is selected	
Click **Next**	To display the first group of options.
3 Observe the settings	These settings are useful for enhancing the appearance of text when viewed with a screen magnifier.
Click **Next**	
4 Observe the settings	These settings are useful for specifying how Acrobat determines the reading order.
Click **Next** and observe the settings	These settings are useful for specifying the number of pages that should be accessed at a time. Sometimes, opening a large document all at once can degrade the performance of assistive devices.
5 Click **Next**	You'll disable the auto-save feature because it can cause some assistive devices to restart reading from the beginning of the document.
6 Check **Disable document auto-save**	You'll also specify that documents you reopen should open to the page you last accessed.
7 Check **Reopen documents to the last viewed page**	
Click **Done**	

Specifying accessibility preferences

Explanation

You can specify accessibility preferences in several categories of the Preferences dialog box. To apply your accessibility preferences:

1   Choose Edit, Preferences to open the Preferences dialog box.

2   Select a category.

3   Specify the accessibility preferences you want to use.

4   Click OK.

The following table describes the accessibility preferences available in several preference categories.

Category	Description
Accessibility	Specify options for document color, tab order, and the selection cursor.
Forms	Select background or highlighting colors for form fields.
Multimedia	Select options for including supplemental content that might be part of multimedia material. You can specify options for showing subtitles, playing dubbed audio, showing supplemental text captions, and showing content descriptions, when available.
Reading	Specify reading order options, screen reader options, and settings for Acrobat's Read Out Loud feature.

You can use Acrobat's Read Out Loud option to have Acrobat read the current PDF document aloud. The Read Out Loud option will read document text, as well as any alternate text specified for figures and other content. Before using the Read Out Loud options, you need to activate it by choosing View, Read Out Loud, Activate Read Out Loud. When you're not using the Read Out Loud feature, you can deactivate it to free up system resources to improve performance for other operations. To deactivate it, choose View, Read Out Loud, Deactivate Read Out Loud.

After activating Read Out Loud, you can use the Read out Loud submenu to control the feature.

* To read a single page, choose View, Read Out Loud, Read This Page Only.
* To read an entire document, choose View, Read Out Loud, Read To End of Document.
* To pause the reading, choose View, Read Out Loud, Pause.
* To stop the reading, choose View, Read Out Loud, Stop.

Do it!

B-2:   Setting reader preferences

Here's how	Here's why
1 Choose **Edit, Preferences...**	To open the Preferences dialog box. You'll customize the preferences for Acrobat's Read Out Loud feature.
In the Categories list, select **Reading**	
2 Read the settings under Reading Order Options and Screen Reader Options	You'll leave these options at their default settings.
3 Under Read Out Loud options, from the Volume list, select **8**	
Click **OK**	You'll test the Read Out Loud option.
4 Open My Add tags.pdf	
5 Choose **View, Read Out Loud, Activate Read Out Loud**	To activate the Read Out Loud feature.
6 Choose **View, Read Out Loud, Read This Page Only**	Acrobat begins reading the document text, as well as the alternate text you specified earlier for the two figures.
7 Choose **View, Read Out Loud, Stop**	(If necessary.) To stop the Read Out Loud audio.
8 Choose **View, Read Out Loud, Deactivate Read Out Loud**	To disable the feature, freeing up system resources so that other operations can function more efficiently.
9 Close the file	

Unit summary: PDF accessibility

Topic A

In this topic, you learned how to **apply tags** to a PDF document. You also learned how to check for potential **accessibility** problems and fix those problems. Then you learned how to modify a tagged document's **reading order**, and you learned how to create a new **tag structure** for a PDF document.

Topic B

In this topic, you learned how to use the **Setup Accessibility Assistant** to customize accessibility preferences in the Acrobat environment. You also learned how to customize **accessibility preferences**, and use the **Read Out Loud** feature to access PDF content.

Independent practice activity

In this activity, you'll add tags to a document and perform a full accessibility check. You'll specify a document's language and you'll add alternate text for a graphic. Finally, you'll adjust accessibility preferences and use the Read Out Loud feature.

1 Open Accessibility practice.pdf from the current unit folder.

2 Save the file as **My Accessibility practice**.

3 Determine whether or not this is a tagged document. (*Hint*: Choose **File**, **Properties**, activate the Description tag, and observe the Tagged PDF status.)

4 Add tags to the document. (*Hint*: Choose **Advanced**, **Accessibility**, **Add Tags to Document**.)

5 Save the document and perform a full accessibility check. (*Hint*: Choose **Advanced**, **Accessibility**, **Full Check**.)

6 Observe the instructions in the Accessibility Report, and set the document's language to English.

7 Specify appropriate alternate text for the logo at the top of page 1.

8 Save the document and run the accessibility Full Check again to verify that there are no remaining accessibility issues.

9 Verify that the document's reading order is correct. (*Hint*: Choose **Tools**, **Advanced Editing**, **TouchUp Reading Order Tool**, and in the TouchUp Reading Order dialog box, verify that **Show page content order** is checked.)

10 Close the TouchUp Reading Order dialog box.

11 Set the Read Out Loud volume to **5**. (*Hint*: Choose **Edit**, **Preferences** and select the **Reading** category. From the Volume drop-down list, select **5** and click **OK**.)

12 Have Acrobat begin reading the document aloud; stop it shortly thereafter.

13 Save and close the document.

14 Close any floating palette windows.

Review questions

1 How can you define a document's structure so that it can be interpreted accurately by assistive technologies such as screen readers and screen magnifiers?

A Generate tags, which you can create only from within the document's authoring application.

B Generate tags, which you can create only from within Acrobat.

C Generate tags, which you can create from within the document's authoring application or from within Acrobat.

D Generate tags, which you can create only from within assistive technology software.

2 Which command can you use to generate an accessibility report that you can save as an HTML file on your computer?

A Choose Advanced, Accessibility, Quick Check.

B Choose Advanced, Accessibility, Full Check.

C Choose Advanced, Accessibility, Create Report.

D Choose Advanced, Accessibility, Setup Assistant.

3 How can you make a graphic accessible?

A Tag the graphic with the <Text> tag.

B Tag the graphic with the <Figure> tag.

C Remove the <Figure> tag associated with the graphic.

D Add alternate text for the graphic's <Figure> tag in the TouchUp Properties dialog box.

4 How can you change the reading order in a tagged PDF document?

A Use the Select tool to drag highlighted regions to rearrange them; then choose Advanced, Accessibility, Refresh Reading Order.

B In the TouchUp Reading Order dialog box, click Show Order Panel, and in the Order panel, drag the icon for an item to rearrange it in the reading order.

C In the Tags panel, drag the icon for an item to rearrange it in the document's structure.

D Select the TouchUp Reading Order tool, and click each highlighted region in the order that you want them to appear in the reading order.

5 If you use a screen reader or screen magnifier, how can you specify settings you want to use on your system for accessing PDF content?

A Choose Advanced, Accessibility, Setup Assistant.

B Choose Advanced, Accessibility, Full Check.

C Choose Advanced, Accessibility, Structure Content.

D Choose Advanced, Accessibility, Enable Accessibility.

Unit 6

Document security

Unit time: 75 minutes

Complete this unit, and you'll know how to:

A Secure a PDF document by applying a password that's required to open the document.

B Create and export digital IDs, digitally sign PDF documents, and validate signatures.

C Encrypt PDF files based on user certificates.

D Encrypt PDF files by using Adobe LiveCycle Policy Server.

E Create password and certificate security policies.

Topic A: Password protection

This topic covers the following ACE exam objective for Acrobat 8.0 Professional.

#	Objective
7.1	List and describe methods that can be used to secure a PDF document by using passwords.

Basic document security

Explanation

Acrobat makes it easy to protect your documents from unauthorized use. You can disallow anyone without a password from opening a PDF document. You can also restrict anyone without the proper password from printing, copying, or modifying the document.

The Password Security – Settings dialog box

You can specify password protection by using the Password Security – Settings dialog box, shown in Exhibit 6-1.

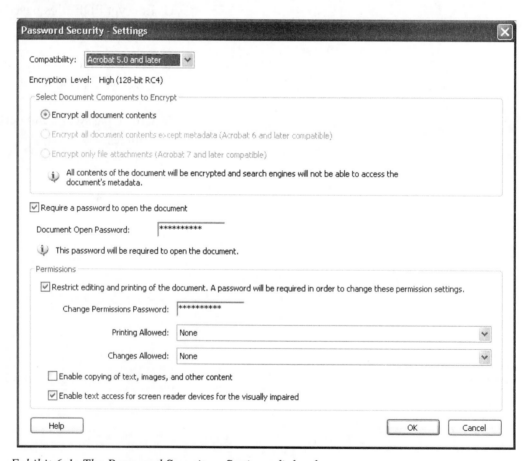

Exhibit 6-1: The Password Security – Settings dialog box

You use this dialog box to specify a *Document Open password*, a *Permissions password*, or both. If a PDF document uses a Document Open password, a dialog box appears when someone attempts to open the file. In this dialog box, the user must enter the correct password to open the file. If a document uses a Permissions password, then certain tasks, such as printing or editing, will be prohibited.

To set a Document Open password:

1 Open the PDF file you want to protect.

2 On the Tasks toolbar, click Secure, and from the menu that appears, choose Show Security Properties. The Document Properties dialog box opens with the Security tab activated.

3 From the Security Method list, select Password Security to open the Password Security – Settings dialog box.

4 Check Require a password to open the document.

5 In the Document Open Password box, enter the password you want to use and click OK. The Confirm Document Open Password dialog box appears.

6 In the Document Open Password box, enter the password you specified and click OK. A dialog box appears, indicating that the security settings you specified won't take effect until you save and close the file.

7 Click OK to return to the Document Properties dialog box.

8 Click OK.

Do it!

A-1: Setting a Document Open password

Here's how	Here's why
1 Open Progress report.pdf	(From the current unit folder.) You'll specify a Document Open password.
Save the file as **My Progress report**	
2 On the Tasks toolbar, click 🔒 Secure ▾	To display the Secure menu.
Choose **Show Security Properties...**	To open the Document Properties dialog box. The Security tab is activated.
3 From the Security Method list, select **Password Security**	To open the Password Security – Settings dialog box.
4 Check **Require a password to open the document**	
Type **openpassword**	(In the Document Open Password box.) To open this document, you'll need to enter this password.
Click **OK**	The Adobe Acrobat – Confirm Document Open Password dialog box appears.
5 Type **openpassword**	
Click **OK**	(To confirm the password.) A security dialog box appears, indicating that the settings won't take effect until you save the file.
Click **OK**	To return to the Document Properties dialog box.
Click **OK**	
6 Save and close the file	
7 Open My Progress report.pdf	The Password dialog box appears.
Type **openpassword**	
Click **OK**	To open the file.

Permissions passwords

You can use a Permissions password to prohibit certain tasks, such as printing or editing. If you want to perform a prohibited action, you have to change the document's security settings, which you'll be able to do only if you know the Permissions password.

To set a Permissions password:

1 Open the PDF file that you want to protect.

2 On the Tasks toolbar, click Secure and choose Show Security Properties. The Document Properties dialog box opens with the Security tab activated.

3 Open the Password Security – Settings dialog box.

- If you haven't already set any security settings for this document, then from the Security Method list, select Password Security.

- If you've already specified security settings for this document and you don't want to replace them, then you can modify them by clicking Change Settings.

4 Under Permissions, check Restrict editing and printing of the document.

5 In the Change Permissions Password box, enter the password you want to use.

6 Under Permissions, specify the restrictions you want to apply:

- From the Printing Allowed drop-down list, specify if you want to prohibit printing, allow low-resolution printing, or allow high-resolution printing.

- From the Changes Allowed drop-down list, specify the types of editing changes you want to allow.

- Check or clear Enable copying of text, images, and other content.

- Check or clear Enable text access for screen reader devices for the visually impaired.

7 Click OK. A dialog box opens, indicating that Adobe products support the security settings you're applying, but that some third-party products might not support all the security settings.

8 Click OK. The Confirm Permissions Password dialog box appears.

9 In the Permissions Password box, enter the password you specified and click OK. A dialog box appears, indicating that the security settings you specified won't take effect until you save and close the file.

10 Click OK to close the Document Properties dialog box.

If you apply both a Document Open password and a Permissions password, you must use a different password for each one.

A-2:   Setting a Permissions password

Here's how	Here's why
1 Click	
Choose **Show Security Properties...**	To open the Document Properties dialog box with the Security tab activated.
2 Click **Change Settings**	To open the Password Security – Settings dialog box. The dialog box shows the Document Open password settings you chose earlier.

3 Under Permissions, check
**Restrict editing and
printing of the document**

In the Change Permissions
Password box, type
editpassword

4 Verify that the Printing Allowed
and Changes Allowed lists are set
to None

5 Verify that Enable copying of
text, images, and other content is
cleared

Click **OK**
An alert dialog box appears, indicating that
Adobe products support the security restrictions
you've specified, but that some third-party PDF
readers might not support them.

Click **OK**
The Confirm Permissions Password dialog box
appears.

6 Type **editpassword**

Click **OK**
An alert dialog box appears, indicating that
these options won't take effect until you save
and close the file.

Click **OK**
You return to the Document Properties dialog
box.

7 Click **OK**

8 Save and close the file
Anyone opening this file will now be unable to
print or modify the document.

9 Open My Progress report.pdf
The Password dialog box appears. You can enter
either the Document Open password or the
Permissions password.

Type **openpassword**

Click **OK**
To open the file.

10 Observe the Print button on the
File toolbar
The Print button and the File menu's Print
command are dimmed, indicating that they're
disabled.

Overriding permissions restrictions

Explanation

When you open a permissions-protected document, certain editing and printing options might not be available. If you want to override the restrictions to gain full access to all commands, you'll need to turn off the permissions settings you want to override. To do so, you'll need to enter the Permissions password.

If a document uses both a Document Open password and a Permissions password, you can open the document using either password. However, you can use only the Permissions password to override the permissions restrictions.

Do it!

A-3: Changing settings in a permissions-protected file

Here's how	Here's why
1 Choose **Tools**, **Advanced Editing**	To view the contents of the Advanced Editing submenu. Most of the items are dimmed.
Click away from the menu	To close it without selecting a command. You'll now modify the permissions settings to allow printing.
2 Click [🔒 Secure ▾]	
Select **Show Security Properties...**	To open the Document Properties dialog box with the Security tab activated.
3 Click **Change Settings**	The Passwords dialog box appears because you can't modify the security settings unless you know the Permissions password.
Type **editpassword** and click **OK**	To open the Password Security – Settings dialog box. The dialog box shows the password settings you chose earlier.
4 From the Printing Allowed list, select **High Resolution**	
Click **OK** three times	To close each dialog box, until you return to the Document Properties dialog box.
Click **OK**	
5 Observe the Print button on the File toolbar	The Print button is no longer disabled. You can now print, although the other permissions restrictions remain in effect.
6 Save and close the file	

Topic B: Digital signatures

This topic covers the following ACE exam objectives for Acrobat 8.0 Professional.

#	Objective
7.2	List and describe the methods available for creating and acquiring digital signatures and certificates.
7.3	Certify a document by applying a digital signature.

Signatures and IDs

Explanation

You can use a *digital signature* in much the same way you use a handwritten signature. Either kind of signature identifies the signer. A digital signature stores data about the signer that uniquely identifies that person, much like a handwritten signature's unique appearance identifies the signer.

Digital IDs

Before you can digitally sign a document, you need to create a *digital ID* that uniquely identifies you. You can then distribute that digital ID to people to whom you'll send digitally signed files. Those recipients can verify the authenticity of your digitally signed documents by comparing them to your digital ID of record.

To create a digital ID:

1   Choose Advanced, Security Settings to open the Security Settings window.
2   Select Digital IDs to display the Digital ID settings.
3   Click Add ID to open the Add Digital ID wizard.
4   Select Create a self-signed digital ID for use with Acrobat.
5   Click Next.
6   Select how you want to store the digital ID and click Next.

- Select New PKCS#12 digital ID file to create a digital ID file that uses the standard PKCS#12 format, which is supported by most security software programs.

- Select Windows Certificate Store to store the digital ID file in the Windows Certificate Store, which will make it available to other Windows applications.

7   Specify options for the identity information included in your digital ID and click Next.
8   In the Password and Confirm Password boxes, enter the password you want to use. You'll have to enter this password each time you sign a document.
9   Click Finish to complete the digital ID. The new digital ID appears in the Security Settings window, as shown in Exhibit 6-2. You can now close the Security Settings window, or export a digital ID certificate file to distribute to people to whom you plan to send digitally signed documents.

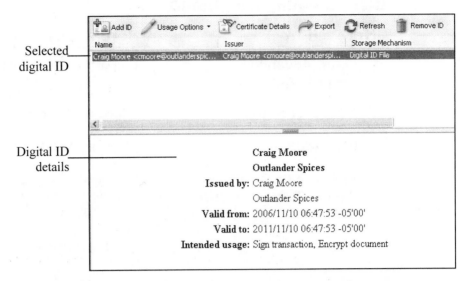

Selected digital ID

Digital ID details

Exhibit 6-2: A digital ID shown in the Security Settings window

B-1:   Creating a digital ID

Here's how	Here's why
1 Choose **Advanced, Security Settings...**	To open the Security Settings window.
Select **Digital IDs**	(If necessary.) To display the Digital ID settings.
2 Click **Add ID**	To open the Add Digital ID wizard.
Select **Create a self-signed digital ID for use with Acrobat**	To create a digital ID and certificate that you can share with others so they can validate your digital signatures.
Click **Next**	To display options for how your digital ID is stored.
3 Select **New PKCS#12 digital ID file**	(If necessary.) To specify a password-protected digital ID file that uses the PKCS#12 format.
Click **Next**	To display options for the identity information used when generating the self-signed certificate.
4 In the Name box, enter your name	
In the Organization Name box, enter **Outlander Spices**	
In the Email Address box, enter **cmoore@outlanderspices.com**	
Click **Next**	To display settings for specifying the file location and password for your digital ID file.
5 Click **Browse**	To open the Save Digital ID File dialog box.
Navigate to the current unit folder and click **Save**	To specify the location for the new digital ID.
6 In the Password box, enter **password**	
In the Confirm Password box, enter **password**	
Click **Finish**	To create your digital ID and return to the Security Settings dialog box.
7 Select your digital ID	(In the list of digital IDs.) To display the digital ID details.

Sharing digital ID certificate files

Explanation

After you create a digital ID, you can export it as a digital ID certificate file. You can distribute that file to everyone to whom you'll send digitally signed documents so they can use it to authenticate your signed documents.

To export a digital ID as a digital ID certificate file:

1 Choose Advanced, Security settings to open the Security Settings window.
2 Select your digital ID.
3 Click Export to open the Data Exchange File – Export Options dialog box.
4 Select Save the data to a file, then click Next to open the Export Data As dialog box. The file is named CertExchange<your name>.
5 Navigate to the folder in which you want to save the digital ID certificate file, and click Save.
6 If an alert dialog box appears, click OK.
7 Distribute the digital ID certificate file to everyone to whom you plan to send digitally signed documents.

Do it!

B-2:   Exporting a digital ID certificate file

Here's how	Here's why
1 Select your digital ID	(If necessary.) In the Security Settings window. You'll export your digital ID certificate file so you can provide it to people who will use it to validate your digital signatures.
2 Click **Export**	To open the Data Exchange File – Export Options dialog box.
3 Select **Save the data to a file**	If necessary.
Click **Next**	To open the Export Data As dialog box.
4 Observe the File Name box	The file name is CertExchange<your name>.
5 Navigate to the current unit folder and click **Save**	To save the certificate file. An Acrobat Security dialog box appears.
Click **OK**	
6 Close the Security Settings window	Now you can e-mail or otherwise distribute the certificate file to anyone who might need to validate one of your digital signatures.

Digitally signing PDF documents

Explanation

After you've created a digital ID, you can digitally sign PDF documents by using Acrobat. To digitally sign a PDF document:

1 On the Tasks toolbar, click Sign, and choose Place Signature. A dialog box displays instructions for dragging where you want to add the signature.

2 Click OK.

3 Drag where you want the signature to appear on the document. The Sign Document dialog box appears.

4 If you have multiple digital IDs, then from the Digital ID list, select the digital ID you want.

5 In the Password box, enter the password you specified for your digital ID.

6 Click Sign. The Save As dialog box appears so you can save the signed copy of the PDF document.

7 Specify a name for the document and click Save. The signature appears on the document.

8 Click the signature on the document to display the Signature Validation Status dialog box; then click Close.

Do it!

B-3: Digitally signing a PDF document

Here's how	Here's why
1 Open Confidential memo.pdf	From the current unit folder. You'll digitally sign this document.
2 Click [Sign ▾]	(On the Tasks toolbar.) To display the Sign menu.
Choose **Place Signature...**	(From the Sign menu.) A dialog box appears with instructions for dragging to add the digital signature.
Click **OK**	You can now drag to specify the size and location of the digital signature.
3 Drag to add the digital signature, as shown	**Confidential Memo** TO: Senior Management When you release the mouse button, the Sign Document dialog box appears.
4 Verify that the Digital ID box displays your digital ID	
5 In the Confirm Password box, enter **password**	

6 Click **Sign**

The Save As dialog box appears so you can save the signed version of the document.

   Navigate to the current unit folder

If necessary.

   Name the file
   My signed memo

   Click **Save**

Your digital signature appears where you dragged.

7 Observe your digital signature on the document

A green checkmark appears, indicating that your signature is valid.

8 Use the Hand tool to click the signature

To display the Signature Validation Status dialog box, which indicates that the signature is valid.

   Click **Close**

9 Close the file

Validating signed documents

Explanation

When someone sends you a PDF document that they've digitally signed, you'll need to validate the authenticity of the signature. To do so, you'll need a digital ID certificate file from that person that you can compare to the signed document. You keep digital ID certificate files in a list of trusted identities within Acrobat. When you open a digitally signed document, the signature in the document is automatically compared to your list of trusted identities for validation.

To import a digital ID certificate file as a trusted identity:

1 Choose Advanced, Manage Trusted Identities to open the Manage Trusted Identities dialog box.

2 Click Add Contacts to open the Choose Contacts to Import dialog box.

3 Click Browse, navigate to and select the PDF file containing the digital certificate, and click Open.

4 Under Contacts, select the certificate you added so that it also appears under Certificates. Under Certificates, select the certificate and click Details to open the Certificate Viewer dialog box.

5 Activate the Details tab and observe the SHA-1 and MD5 fingerprint numbers. Contact the person who sent you the certificate file, and confirm that these numbers represent that person's authentic signature data. Click OK.

6 Under Certificate, select the certificate and click Trust to open the Import Contact Settings dialog box. Check the check boxes reflecting how you want to use the digital certificate and click OK.

7 In the Choose Contacts to Import dialog box, click Import. When a dialog box indicates that the certificate was added as a trusted identity, click OK.

8 Close the Manage Trusted Identities dialog box.

Do it!

B-4: Validating a signed document

Here's how	Here's why
1 Open Check signature.pdf	
	This document was signed by J Barclay, but a question mark appears on the signature, indicating that the signer's identity is unknown.
Close the file	You'll import a digital ID certificate for this person so that you can authenticate the signature. (You already have the digital ID certificate file stored on your computer.)
2 Choose **Advanced**, **Manage Trusted Identities...**	To open the Manage Trusted Identities dialog box.
3 Click **Add Contacts**	To open the Choose Contacts to Import dialog box.
4 Click **Browse**	To open the Locate Certificate File dialog box.
Select **CertExchangeJBarclay.fdf**	(In the current unit folder.) This is the certificate file for J Barclay.
Click **Open**	To add the certificate file to the Contacts list.
5 Under Contacts, click **JBarclay**	The JBarclay certificate now appears under Certificates.
6 Under Certificates, click **JBarclay** and click **Details**	To open the Certificate Viewer dialog box for this file.
Activate the Details tab and scroll down	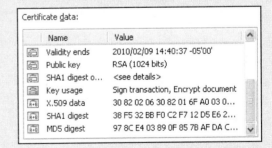
	To observe the SHA-1 and MD5 fingerprint numbers. You could now contact J Barclay to verify that these numbers are correct.
Click **OK**	
7 Under Certificates, click **Trust**	To open the Import Contact Settings dialog box.

8	Under Trust, check **Signatures and as a trusted root**	
	Click **OK**	To return to the Choose Contacts to Import dialog box.
9	Click **Import**	The Import Complete dialog box appears.
	Click **OK**	JBarclay now appears in your list of trusted identities in the Manage Trusted Identities dialog box.
10	Click **Close**	You'll now open the signed document to validate the signature.
11	Open Check signature.pdf	
		A green checkmark on the signature indicates that the signature is valid.
12	Close the file	

Barclay

Digitally signed by J Barclay
DN: cn=J Barclay, c=US,
o=Outlander Spices
Reason: I am the author of
this document
Date: 2005.02.09 14:41:57
-05'00'

✳ Creating blank signature fields

Explanation   If you're creating a PDF document that you plan to distribute to others, and you want them to digitally sign the document, you might want to add blank digital signature fields in which they can sign. People can sign a PDF document even if it doesn't include a digital signature field, but adding one can make it easier for people to sign the document.

To create a blank digital signature field:

1. Choose Tools, Forms, Digital Signature Tool to select the Digital Signature tool.
2. Drag to specify the location and size of the digital signature field. The Digital Signature Properties dialog box appears.
3. Specify the properties you want the digital signature field to use and click Close.
4. If you want to modify a digital signature field's properties, you can use the Digital Signature tool to double-click the digital signature field to open the Digital Signature Properties dialog box.

The following table describes the tabs in the Digital Signature Properties dialog box.

Tab	Description
General	Specify the digital signature field name, a tooltip (if any), its screen and print visibility, its orientation, its read-only status, and whether it's a required field or not.
Appearance	Specify the field's border and color attributes, as well as its type formatting.
Actions	Specify an action you want to be performed when someone uses the signature field.
Signed	Specify what happens after the field is signed. You can specify that nothing happens, that specified fields are marked as read-only, or that a specified script executes.

When recipients view the PDF file, they can use the Hand tool to click the digital signature field to sign it, or they can click Sign and choose Sign Document.

B-5: Creating a blank digital signature field

Here's how	Here's why
1 Open Certified.pdf	From the current unit folder.
Save the file as **My Certified**	
2 Choose **Tools**, **Forms**, **Digital Signature Tool**	To select the Digital Signature tool.
3 In the top-left corner, drag as shown	
	To specify the signature field's location and basic dimensions. The Digital Signature Properties dialog box opens. Because you added a form field, a message appears at the top of the screen, prompting respondents to fill out the form. You'll hide that message, because you're the form author and don't need to fill it out.
4 Click as shown	
	To hide the form message. You can click the button again to display the message.
5 Activate the General tab	(In the Digital Signature Properties dialog box.) You'll specify a tooltip to appear for the signature field.
In the Tooltip box, enter **Approval signature**	You'll format the field with a black border so viewers will see it easily.
6 Activate the Appearance tab	
Next to Border Color, click the swatch and select a dark color	
7 From the Line Thickness list, select **Medium**	
Click **Close**	To close the dialog box.
8 Select the Hand tool	To deselect the signature field.

9 Point to the signature field

To view the tooltip, which displays the text you specified, along with the words "click to sign."

10 Save your changes

Certifying PDF documents

Explanation

If you want to ensure that a PDF document is not modified after you sign it, you can save the document as a certified document. When you certify a document, you sign it and specify the types of changes that are permitted (if any) for the file to retain its certified status. If someone modifies the file in an unapproved way, the file's certified status is broken.

To certify a PDF file:

1 Finalize any changes to the PDF file.

2 Choose File, Save as Certified Document to open the Save as Certified Document dialog box. You can also click Sign and choose Certify with Visible Signature or choose Certify without Visible Signature.

3 Click OK. If you're adding a visible digital signature, drag to specify the location and dimensions of the visible digital signature. The Certify Document dialog box appears.

4 From the Permitted Changes after Certifying list, specify the types of changes you'll allow while retaining the file's certification status. You can specify that no changes are allowed, that form fill-in and digital signature changes are allowed, or that annotations, form fill-in, and digital signature changes are allowed.

5 Click Sign.

Do it!

B-6: Certifying a PDF document

Here's how	Here's why
1 Choose **File**, **Save as Certified Document...**	To open the Save as Certified Document dialog box. You'll certify this document so that others who open it can verify that you attest to its content, and that the content hasn't been modified since the time that you certified it.
Click **OK**	A dialog box appears, instructing you to draw the digital signature field.
Click **OK**	
2 Drag to draw the digital signature field, as shown	The Certify Document dialog box appears.
3 From the Permitted Changes after Certifying list, select **Form fill-in and digital signatures**	(If necessary.) To prohibit any changes to the document except the filling out of form input fields. In this case, you want to ensure that your recipient can sign the blank digital signature field you created earlier.
In the Password box, type **password**	

4 Click **Sign**

The Save As dialog box appears, so you can save a new copy of the certified document.

Name the file **My certified complete** and click **Save**

A message appears at the top of the window, indicating that you certify the document. You'll now close and reopen the document to see how it will appear to others.

5 Close the file and reopen it

Your signature appears with a blue ribbon icon, indicating that the document is certified.

6 Click your digital signature

(With the Hand tool.) To open the Signature Validation Status dialog box, which indicates that the document certification is valid.

Click **Close**

When you certified this document, you indicated that the only allowable changes are form field entries and digital signatures. All other modifications to this file are prohibited.

7 Click the blank signature field you created earlier

The Sign Document dialog box appears, so you know that the recipient will be able to sign the document.

Click **Cancel**

8 Close the file

Topic C: Encryption certification and security envelopes

This topic covers the following ACE exam objective for Acrobat 8.0 Professional.

#	Objective
7.4	Secure documents by creating a security envelope.

Using certificates to encrypt PDF files

Explanation

In addition to using certificates to verify that a digital signature is valid, you can use certificates to specify a list of individuals who can access encrypted PDF files. When you encrypt a file based on certificate security, only the individuals whose digital IDs match the specified certificates will be able to open the file. You can also specify each recipient's level of access to the file, such as editing or printing permissions.

When you encrypt a PDF file using certificates, you must begin by specifying your own digital ID to ensure that you'll be able to access the file after encrypting it.

To encrypt a PDF file based on certificates:

1 On the Tasks toolbar, click the Secure button to display the menu, and choose Show Security Properties. The Document Properties dialog box opens with the Security tab activated.

2 From the Security Method list, select Certificate Security to open the Certificate Security Settings wizard.

3 Specify general settings and click Next. The Document Security – Digital ID Selection dialog box opens.

4 Select your own digital ID and click OK to ensure that you'll be able to open the file after you've encrypted it.

5 In the Certificate Security Settings dialog box, your digital ID is listed as a recipient. Click Browse and navigate to and select the certificates of users to whom you want to grant access to the file.

6 Select one or more names in the recipients list, click Permissions, specify any restrictions, and click OK.

7 Click Next to view a summary of the settings you specified.

8 Click Finish.

9 Click OK to close the Document Properties dialog box.

Do it!

C-1:   Encrypting a PDF file by using a certificate

Here's how	Here's why
1 Open Certificate security.pdf	(From the current unit folder.) You'll encrypt this file so that only one other person can open it.
Save the file as **My Certificate security**	
2 Click [🔒 Secure ▾]	On the Tasks toolbar.
Choose **Show Security Properties...**	To open the Document Properties dialog box with the Security tab activated.
3 From the Security Method list, select **Certificate Security**	The Certificate Security Settings wizard appears.
Verify that **Discard these settings after applying** is selected	You won't save these security settings as a policy for use with future files you encrypt.
Verify that **Encrypt all document contents** is selected	To encrypt the document, including any attachments and metadata. When metadata is encrypted, search engines can't access it.
4 Verify that **128-bit AES** is specified	In the Encryption Algorithm list.
Click **Next**	You'll add the certificate for J Barclay to the list of recipients.
5 Click **Browse...**	The Locate Certificate File dialog box opens.
Select **CertExchangeJBarclay**, and click **Open**	(In the current unit folder.) To add the certificate for J Barclay to the list of recipients who will be able to open this file. Next, you'll specify restrictions for how J Barclay can use the file.
6 In the list of recipients, click **J Barclay**, and then click **Permissions...**	An alert dialog box appears, warning you that some third party PDF viewers might not fully support the security settings you specify.
Click **OK**	The Permission Settings dialog box opens.

7 Check **Restrict printing and editing of the document and its security settings**

From the Printing allowed list, verify that **None** is selected	To ensure that J Barclay can't print the file.
From the Changes allowed list, select **Commenting, filling in form fields, and signing existing signature fields**	To enable J Barclay to review the document without changing the document content.
Clear both check boxes at the bottom	To restrict J Barclay from copying content or accessing the material with a screen reader or other assistive device.
Click **OK**	To close the Acrobat Security box.
Click **OK**	

8 Click **Next**, and then click **Finish** — An alert dialog box appears, indicating that the security settings won't take effect until you save the file.

Click **OK**	

9 Click **OK** — To close the Document Properties dialog box.

10 Save and close the file

Open My Certificate security.pdf	The Digital ID Authentication dialog box appears. You must enter the password associated with your digital ID.
In the Password box, enter **password** and click **OK**	To open the file. You didn't specify any restrictions for yourself, so you can continue to modify the file any way you want. However, J Barclay would be restricted based on the settings you specified.
Close the file	

✍ **Security envelopes**

Explanation

Sometimes you might need to send multiple secured files to a recipient. Instead of applying encryption settings to each document, you can create a security envelope (as shown in Exhibit 6-3), and attach the files within it. When recipients open the encrypted security envelope, they can extract the attached documents without any encryption settings applied to them directly.

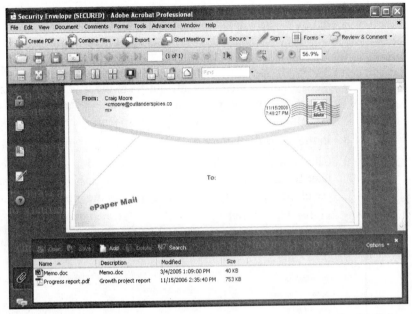

Exhibit 6-3: An example of a security envelope with two embedded documents

To attach documents in a security envelope:

1 On the Tasks toolbar, click Secure and choose Create Security Envelope. The Create Security Envelope wizard appears, as shown in Exhibit 6-4.

2 Click Add File To Send to open the Files to Enclose dialog box. Navigate to the documents you want to include, select them, and then click Open.

3 Click Next to move to the next panel in the wizard.

4 Under Available Templates, select an envelope template and click Next.

5 Select a delivery method and click Next.

6 Check Show All Policies, and then select a security policy from the list. You can also create a new policy by clicking the New Policy button. Click Next.

7 Verify that the envelope attributes are the way you want them, and click Finish. Depending on the type of security policy you applied to the envelope, a corresponding security dialog box appears.

8 In the security dialog box, enter the required information and click OK.

9 Click OK to finish the wizard. If you opted to send the security envelope at a later time, you can attach it to an e-mail message. If you opted to send the envelope right away, type an address in the message that appears and click Send.

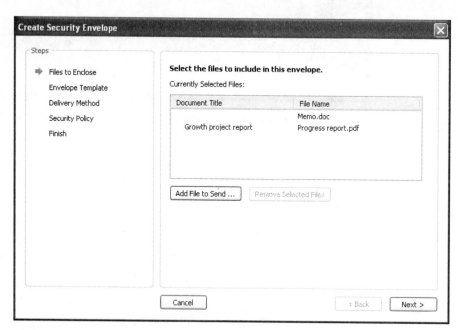

Exhibit 6-4: The first panel in the Security Envelope wizard

Do it!

C-2: Creating a security envelope

Here's how	Here's why
1 Click Secure ▾	
Choose **Create Security Envelope...**	To open the Create Security Envelope wizard.
2 Click **Add File to Send...**	To open the Files to Enclose dialog box.

3	Navigate to the current unit folder and select **Memo.doc**	
	Press and hold CTRL and select **Progress report.pdf**	To select both documents.
	Click **Open**	The two documents are listed in the wizard.
4	Click **Next**	To move to the next pane in the wizard.
5	Under Available Templates, select **eEnvelope with Date Stamp**	
6	Click **Next**	
7	Verify that **Send the envelope later** is selected, and click **Next**	
8	Check **Show all policies**	
	Select **Password Encrypt…**	
9	Click **Next**	
	Click **Next**	A security dialog box appears. You'll ignore this for now.
	Click **OK**	To close the Acrobat Security box.
10	Click **Finish**	The Password Security – Settings dialog box appears.
11	Check **Require password to open document**	
	In the Document Open Password box, type **openpassword**	
	Click **OK**	The Adobe Acrobat – Confirm Document Open Password dialog box appears.
12	Type **openpassword**	In the alert dialog box's Document Open Password box.
	Click **OK**	A security dialog box appears, indicating that the settings won't take effect until you save the file.
	Click **OK**	
13	Save the envelope as **Security Envelope**	In the current unit folder.
	Close the envelope	

Topic D: Adobe LiveCycle Policy Server encryption

This topic covers the following ACE exam objective for Acrobat 8.0 Professional.

#	Objective
7.5	Describe the functionality provided by Adobe LiveCycle Policy Server for encrypting PDF documents.

Encrypting PDF files by using Adobe LiveCycle Policy Servers

Explanation

Another way you can encrypt a PDF document is by using *Adobe LiveCycle Policy Server*, a Web-based security system that allows you to control document security dynamically. With Adobe LiveCycle Policy Server, you set up Web-based PDF document security policies to secure specific PDF documents. The security policies are stored on an Adobe LiveCycle Policy Server. When a user attempts to open a secured document, the policy is retrieved from the Adobe LiveCycle Policy Server, and the user must authenticate his or her identity before opening the file. The user can then use the file only as specified by the policy.

In addition, the policy can be changed at any time. For example, the policy could be revoked immediately, removing the ability for users to access the file. A policy can also be set to cause a PDF file to expire on a given date.

To use an Adobe LiveCycle Policy Server, your organization must purchase rights to use it. After purchasing rights, a system administrator in your organization can configure Adobe LiveCycle Policy Server and set up policies on the Adobe LiveCycle Policy Server. An author can then create a file and apply a policy from the Adobe LiveCycle Policy Server. Finally, a user can open the file, authenticate his or her identity to decrypt it, and use the file based on the permissions specified by the policy. The PDF author or system administrator can use the Web Console to track events and change access to the document.

You must log on to an Adobe LiveCycle Policy Server to use the policies stored there. To log in to an Adobe LiveCycle Policy Server:

1 Choose Advanced, Security Settings to open the Security Settings dialog box.
2 In the list on the left, select Adobe LiveCycle Policy Servers.
3 Click the New button.
4 In the Name box, enter a name, and in the Server Name box, enter the appropriate URL.
5 In the Port box, enter the appropriate port number.
6 Specify the user name and password for your account, and click OK.

To view Adobe LiveCycle Policy Server policies:

1 On the Tasks toolbar, click the Secure button and choose Adobe Policy Server, Manage My Account.

2 Enter your user name and password, if necessary, and click Login.

3 On the Adobe LiveCycle Policy Server page that opens in your Web browser, click Policies.

To create a security policy by using the Adobe LiveCyclePolicy Server:

1 Choose Advanced, Security, Manage Security Policies.

2 Click New to open the New Security Policy dialog box.

3 Select Use The Adobe LiveCycle Policy Server and click Next. This option is available only if your organization has access to the Adobe Policy Server.

4 On the Adobe LiveCycle Policy Server Web page that opens in your browser, click Policies.

5 Click New.

6 Specify the policy name, description, validity period, and other options.

7 Click OK.

8 Specify encryption settings and specify whether you want a watermark.

9 Click Save.

Do it!

D-1: Discussing Adobe LiveCycle Policy Server encryption

Question	Answer
1 When you use Adobe LiveCycle Policy Server, where is the security policy stored for a given PDF file?	
2 What are some ways that Adobe LiveCycle Policy Server can make a document secure?	
3 In what way is Adobe LiveCycle Policy Server more flexible than other types of PDF document security?	
4 What must you do before you can use the policies stored on an Adobe LiveCycle Policy Server?	

Topic E: Password and certificate security policies

Using security policies to manage security

Explanation

In addition to creating security policies that are stored on the Adobe LiveCycle Policy Server, you can also create *password security policies* and *certificate security policies*. If you regularly use the same password security settings or certificate security settings for your documents, you can create policies that store those settings so that you can apply them more efficiently. The password and certificate security policies you specify are stored on your local computer.

You can create security policies by choosing settings in the Manage Security Settings dialog box. To create a password security policy:

1   On the Tasks toolbar, click the Secure button and choose Manage Security Policies.

2   Click New to open the New Security Policy dialog box.

3   Select Use passwords and click Next.

4   Enter a name and description for the policy, and specify whether you want to save a password with the policy. If you don't save a password as part of the policy, you can specify a unique password each time you apply this policy to a document.

5   Click Next.

6   Specify encryption and permissions settings, and click Next. If you specified a password with the policy, you can specify an open password or permissions password.

7   Click Next, and then click Finish to return to the Managing Security Policies dialog box. By default, a yellow star appears next to the new policy, indicating that it will be listed directly in the Secure menu on the Tasks toolbar. You can select a policy and click Favorite to add or remove the policy from the Secure menu. All policies are always available in the Managing Security Policies dialog box.

To create a certificate security policy:

1   On the Tasks toolbar, click the Secure button and choose Manage Security Policies.

2   Click New to open the New Security Policy dialog box.

3   Select Use public key certificates and click Next.

4   Enter a name and description for the policy, specify document components to encrypt, and specify whether you want to be prompted to specify recipients whenever you apply the policy, or whether you want to save the recipients list as part of the policy.

5   Click Next. If you cleared Ask for recipients when applying this policy, you'll be prompted to create the recipients list so that it can be stored with the policy. Specify the recipients list and click Next.

6 Click Finish to return to the Managing Security Policies dialog box. By default, a yellow star appears next to the new policy, indicating that it will be listed directly in the Secure menu on the Tasks toolbar. You can select a policy and click Favorite to add or remove the policy from the Secure menu. All policies are always available in the Managing Security Policies dialog box.

Do it!

E-1: Creating a password security policy

Here's how	Here's why
1 Click [🔒 Secure ▾]	
Choose **Manage Security Policies...**	To open the Managing Security Policies dialog box. You'll create a password security policy using settings that you plan to apply regularly to your PDF documents.
2 Click **New**	(In the top-left corner.) To open the New Security Policy dialog box.
3 Select **Use passwords**	If necessary.
Click **Next**	To display the General settings for creating a password security policy.
4 In the Policy name box, type **Outlander Password Security**	
In the Description box, type **This policy restricts file opening using standard Outlander passwords**	
Check **Save passwords with the policy**	(If necessary.) To specify passwords that will always apply to documents that use this policy.
Click **Next**	To display the Document restrictions settings.
5 Check **Require a password to open the document**	
In the Document Open Password box, type **password**	To specify the password that this policy will apply to any documents that use this policy.
Click **Next**	An Acrobat Security dialog box appears.
6 Type **password** and press **OK**	To confirm the password.
7 Observe the policy details in the dialog box	
Click **Finish**	To return to the Managing Security Policies dialog box. A gold star appears next to the policy, indicating that it's a favorite and will be listed directly in the Secure menu.
8 Click **Close**	

Applying security policies

Explanation

After you create a password or certificate security policy, you can apply it to any PDF document. Security policies you designate as "Favorites" are added to the Secure menu in the Tasks toolbar. You can apply a "Favorite" security policy directly from that menu, or you can apply any security policy by selecting it from within the Managing Security Policies dialog box by using these steps:

1 On the Tasks toolbar, click the Secure button to display the menu, and choose Manage Security Policies to open the Managing Security Policies dialog box.

2 In the list of policies, select the policy you want to apply to the current PDF file.

3 Click Apply to Document and complete any other settings as prompted.

Do it!

E-2: Applying a security policy

Here's how	Here's why
1 Open Security policies.pdf	(From the current unit folder.) You'll apply the new policy you created to this file.
Save the file as **My Security policies**	
2 Click [Secure ▾]	
Choose **Outlander Password Security**	A dialog box appears, asking you to confirm that you want to apply the policy.
Click **Yes**	To confirm that you want to apply the policy to the current file.
Click **OK**	
3 Save and close the file	
4 Open My Security policies.pdf	The Password dialog box appears.
5 In the Enter Password box, enter **password** and click **OK**	To open the file.
6 Close the file	

Unit summary: Document security

Topic A   In this topic, you learned how to specify a **Document Open password** that's required for opening a PDF document. You also learned how to create a **Permissions password** to restrict document printing and editing.

Topic B   In this topic, you created a **digital ID** and exported a **digital ID certificate** file. You also learned how to add your **digital signature** to a PDF document. Finally, you added a digital ID certificate file to your list of **trusted identities**, and used it to **validate** a signed document.

Topic C   In this topic, you learned how to **encrypt** PDF files based on **certificates** so that only users with corresponding **digital IDs** can access the files. You also created **a security envelope** so that you can send a group of files to a recipient without having to apply encryption settings to each file.

Topic D   In this topic, you learned how to **encrypt** PDF files by using **policies** stored on an **Adobe LiveCycle Policy Server**.

Topic E   In this topic, you learned how to create **password security policies** and **certificate security policies**.

Independent practice activity

In this activity, you'll create a password security policy and apply it to a PDF file. You'll also create a self-signed digital ID and export a digital ID certificate file. Finally, you'll digitally sign a document.

1 Create a password security policy named **No editing** that disallows printing, editing, and copying content, and uses **password** as its password.

2 Open Password practice.pdf from the current unit folder.

3 Save the file as **My Password practice**.

4 Apply the **No editing** security policy to the file. (*Hint*: Choose **Secure, No editing**.)

5 Save and close the file, and reopen it to test the password. Click the File menu to verify that the Print command is unavailable.

6 Remove the No editing security settings. (*Hint*: Click **Secure** and choose **Remove Security**.)

7 Create a new self-signed digital ID using the name **Chris Simms** with the e-mail address **csimms@outlanderspices.com**, and use **password** as the password. (*Hint*: Choose **Advanced, Security Settings** to open the Security Settings dialog box.)

8 Export a digital ID certificate file.

9 Digitally sign the My password practice file as Chris Simms, saving the file as **Signing practice**.

10 Close all open documents.

Review questions

1 Which of these actions can be restricted by a permissions password? (Choose all that apply.)

   A Opening the file

   B Printing

   C Editing content

   D Copying content

2 Which of these actions can be restricted by a document open password?

   A Opening the file

   B Printing

   C Editing content

   D Copying content

3 Which item is required for digitally signing a document?

   A A signature field

   B A certificate

   C The Digital Signature tool

   D A digital ID

4 How can you save a PDF document as a certified document?

   A Add your digital signature to the file, which always certifies the file.

   B Choose File, Save as Certified Document.

   C On the Tasks toolbar, choose Sign, Place Signature.

   D On the Tasks toolbar, choose Secure, Manage Security Policies.

5 Which type of security policy should you use if you want to specify a list of recipients who can open the encrypted file based on their digital ID data?

   A Password security policy

   B Certificate security policy

   C Signature security policy

   D Dynamic security policy

6 How can you initiate a security envelope?

   A Choose File, Export, Security Envelope.

   B On the Tasks toolbar, click Combine Files and choose Assemble Files in a Security Envelope.

   C Choose Document, Insert Pages. In the dialog box, check Security Envelope.

   D On the Tasks toolbar, click Secure and choose Create Security Envelope.

7 Which type of security policy should you use if you want to be able to dynamically change document security settings even after distributing a file?

   A Password security policy

   B Certificate security policy

   C Adobe LiveCycle Policy Server policy

   D Dynamic security policy

8 When you use Adobe LiveCycle Policy Server, where is the security policy stored for a given PDF file?

   A As an attachment to the PDF file

   B As part of your digital signature within the PDF file

   C As part of your digital ID

   D On the Adobe LiveCycle Policy Server

Unit 7

Document review techniques

Unit time: 75 minutes

Complete this unit, and you'll know how to:

A Prepare a PDF document for review and initiate automated reviews.

B Use editing and markup tools to review a PDF document.

C Create, organize, and view comments from multiple reviewers.

Topic A: Document reviews

This topic covers the following ACE exam objectives for Acrobat 8.0 Professional.

#	Objective
1.1	Describe the benefits and functionality provided by Acrobat Connect.
4.3	Incorporate headers, footers, watermarks, and backgrounds to a PDF document.
4.4	Attach files to a PDF document.
6.1	Given a scenario, describe the methods available for conducting a review, and when you would use that method.
6.3	Explain how to set up an E-mail review of an Adobe PDF document.
6.4	Explain how to set up shared review of an Adobe PDF document.

Preparing PDF documents for review

Explanation

Before you initiate a group document review, you might want to modify your PDF document. For example, you might want to add a few review comments of your own or an attachment to communicate with reviewers. Another commonly used review technique is to add a *watermark* (a background image) to each page that indicates that the document is a draft or review copy.

Attachments

You can add an attachment to a PDF document so that anyone with access to the document can also access the attachment. You can attach any type of file to a PDF document, but others can open the attachment only if they have a program on their computer that can open the attachment's file type. You can use attachments to include such things as instructions or supporting material, or any other document or file that is in some way relevant to the PDF document.

To embed an attachment to a PDF document:

1 Choose Document, Attach a File to open the Add Attachment dialog box.
2 Navigate to the file you want to attach and select it.
3 Click Open.
4 Activate the Attachments panel to view a list of the file's attachments.

Do it!   **A-1:   Adding an attachment**

Here's how	Here's why
1 Open Initiate review.pdf	(From the current unit folder.) You'll add a review checklist document as an attachment.
Save the file as **My Initiate review**	In the current unit folder.
2 Choose **Document**, **Attach a File...**	To open the Add Attachment dialog box.
Navigate to the current unit folder	
Select **Attachment.rtf**	
Click **Open**	To add the file as an attachment. The Attachments panel is activated, and displays an icon for the attached file.
3 In the Navigation pane, click the Attachments icon	To close the Attachments panel.
4 Save the file	

Watermarks and backgrounds

Explanation

Watermarks and *backgrounds* are text or images that you can add to document pages to indicate the document's status. For example, a watermark or background might display the words "DRAFT" or "For Review Only" on each page, as shown in Exhibit 7-1. A watermark overlaps the content on each page, while a background appears behind the content. However, you can reduce the opacity of a watermark so that users can view the content without any difficulty.

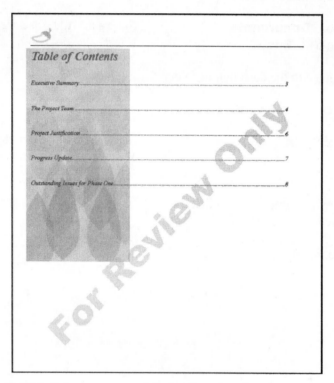

Exhibit 7-1: A watermark indicating that this document is for review only

To add a watermark to a PDF document:

1 Choose Document, Watermark, Add to open the Add Watermark dialog box.

2 Under Source, specify whether you want to create the watermark based on an image or from text you'll enter yourself.

- Select From text, and then type the text you want to use as the watermark or background. Under From text, select the desired formatting options.
- Select From file, and then click Browse. Navigate to and select the file you want to use as the watermark or background.

3 Under Appearance, specify settings to control the watermark's scale, rotation, and opacity.

4 Under Position, specify settings to control the watermark's alignment on the page.

5 To specify the pages on which you want the watermark or background to display, click the Page Range Options link on the right side of the dialog box.

6 Click OK.

To add a background, choose Document, Background, Add, and enter the attributes you want in the Add Background dialog box.

Do it!

A-2:   Adding a watermark

Here's how	Here's why
1 Choose **Document**, **Watermark**, **Add...**	To open the Add Watermark dialog box. You'll add watermark text that displays the words "For Review Only" on each page.
2 Under Source, select **Text**	If necessary.
In the Text box, type **For Review Only**	
From the Font list, select **Arial Black**	
From the Size list, select **72**	The image appears in the dialog box preview.
From the Color list, select a red color	
3 Under Appearance, next to Rotation, select **45°**	To rotate the image 45 degrees.
4 Drag the Opacity slider to about **20%**	
	To lower the image opacity so that it becomes transparent.
5 Click **OK**	To apply the watermark.
6 Activate the Pages panel	
Observe the results	The watermark text appears on every page. The text does not interfere with the readability of the content because the opacity of the watermark text is set very low.
7 Save and close the document	

Initiate reviews

Explanation

You can use Acrobat to initiate or participate in *automated* or *non-automated* reviews. Automated reviews are initiated within Acrobat, and comments are tracked and shared using the Review Tracker. Automated reviews also require that participants use Acrobat 6.0 or later. (Shared reviews require Acrobat 8.0).

Non-automated reviews require that comments be manually e-mailed back to the review initiator, so that he or she can merge the comments with their copy of the PDF. In non-automated reviews, participants can use older versions of Acrobat. The following table describes each review workflow in more detail.

Review type	Description
Shared	A shared review is best for groups that have access to a server. In a shared review, users can add and respond to each other's comments independently. The comments are stored on the server, and are updated each time new comments are published from a local computer. Acrobat then synchronizes the comments with the other local computers included in the review. Viewers can open the PDF being reviewed from any location, but any new comments are saved to the server. All participants must use Acrobat 8.
E-mail-based	An e-mail–based review is one in which the initiator distributes the PDF document vie e-mail. Each participant adds comments and then returns the document by using the Send Comments button in the document message bar. The initiator can then merge the comments into his or her version of the document. A problem with e-mail–based reviews is that participants cannot see each other's comments. All participants must use Acrobat 6 or later.
Browser-based	A browser-based review is one in which reviewers access the PDF document and add comments via their Web browsers. The PDF document is stored in one location on a server, and the reviewer comments are stored in another location. Once the initiator uploads the PDF, he or she sends an e-mail invitation to other participants. The e-mail includes a setup file that opens the PDF in a browser. Reviewers can see the comments made by other participants and can add their own using the available tools. All participants must use Acrobat 6 or later.
Non-automated	A review in which the review initiator will have to use the Import Comments command to import each reviewer's comments into a single PDF document. The PDF document might be distributed via e-mail, but the e-mail applications and Acrobat won't work together to automate any part of the process.

Shared reviews

To initiate a shared review:

1   In the Tasks toolbar, click the Review & Comment button and select Send for Shared Review. The Send PDF for Shared Review wizard opens, as shown in Exhibit 7-2. (You can also choose Comments, Send for Shared Review.)

2   Select a network folder from the Shared Location list, or create a new location by clicking the Add New Location button.

3   Click Next to advance to the next pane in the wizard.

4   Specify whether to send e-mail invitations to reviewers, or to just save the file locally. Click Next.

5   Using the Address Book button, specify the participants you want to include in the review. You can also add participants by typing their e-mail addresses in the Required Viewers or Optional Viewers boxes. Click Next.

6   Customize the e-mail subject and invitation text as necessary and click Finish. Even though participants are invited to join the review via e-mail, their comments will automatically be stored on the server at the location you specified.

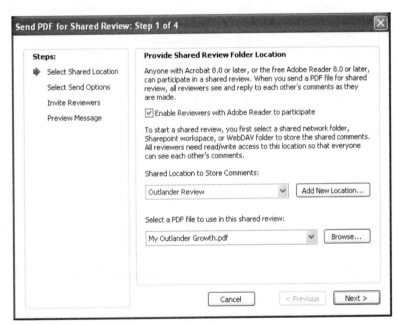

Exhibit 7-2: The first pane in the Send PDF for Shared Review wizard

When you initiate a shared review, a copy of the document is stored at the location on the server you specified. The name of the PDF document has "_Review" added to it. For example, if the shared document was originally called "Outlander Growth.pdf," the shared copy will be saved as "Outlander Growth_Review.pdf" on the server.

E-mail–based reviews

To initiate an e-mail–based review:

1   Click the Review & Comment button and select Attach for Email Review. The Send by Email for Review wizard opens, as shown in Exhibit 7-3.

2   Specify the PDF file you want to send for review from the list, or navigate to the file by using the Browse button. Click Next.

3   Using the Address Book button, specify the participants you want to include in the review. You can also add participants by typing their e-mail addresses in the corresponding box. Separate addresses by using either a semicolon or by pressing Return. Click Next.

4   Verify that the e-mail subject and invitation text is the way you want and click Send Invitation. A copy of the PDF is attached to the e-mail message. When reviewers open the attachment, Acrobat presents commenting tools and a PDF that provides reviewing instructions.

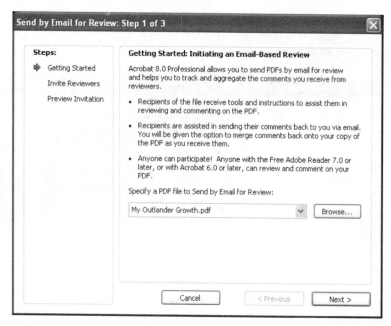

Exhibit 7-3: The first pane in the Send by Email for Review wizard

Browser-based reviews

To initiate a browser-based review:

1 Choose Comments, Upload for Browser Review. The Send PDF for Shared Review wizard opens, as shown in Exhibit 7-4.

2 Specify the PDF file you want to upload for review from the list, or navigate to the file by using the Browse button. Click Next.

3 Specify a location on the server to upload the file. Click Next.

4 Using the Address Book button, specify the participants you want to include in the review. You can also add participants by typing their e-mail addresses in the corresponding box. Separate addresses using either a semicolon or by pressing Return. Click Next.

5 Customize the e-mail subject and invitation text as necessary and click Send Invitation. A copy of the PDF is attached to the e-mail message. When reviewers open the attachment, Acrobat presents commenting tools and a PDF that provides reviewing instructions.

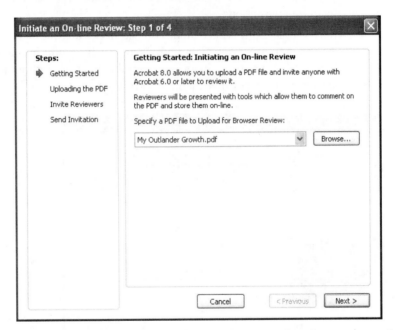

Exhibit 7-4: The first pane in the Initiate an On-line Review wizard

Acrobat Connect

As an alternative to automated reviews, you can also collaborate with others by using Acrobat Connect. Acrobat Connect is adjunct software that allows participants to share screens and participate in real time audio/video conferencing over the Internet. You can launch Acrobat Connect from within Acrobat, but you are required to purchase an Acrobat Connect account if you plan to use the feature on a regular basis. However, before you purchase an account, you might be able to activate a trial account.

To start an Acrobat Connect meeting:

1 Click the Start Meeting button to open the Welcome to Start Meeting dialog box, shown in Exhibit 7-5. You can also Choose File, Start Meeting.

2 Do one of the following:

- If you have an Acrobat Connect account, click Log In. Type the Meeting URL, login, and password, and then click Log In. Your Acrobat Connect account uses your Adobe ID (your e-mail address) for your login.

- If you do not have an account, click Create Trial Account and follow the on-screen instructions.

3 After your account is activated, you can invite anyone with an Internet connection to join your meeting by sending an e-mail invitation from within Acrobat Connect. Participants can join the meeting without requiring any additional software other than their browser.

Exhibit 7-5: The Welcome to Start Meeting dialog box

Do it!

A-3: Discussing automated reviews

Questions and answers

1 Which three review workflows are initiated from within Acrobat?

SHARED REVIEW, E-MAIL BASED & BROWSER REVIEW

2 How can you initiate a shared review?

CLICK REVIEW & COMMENT, SEND FOR SHARED REVIEW
OR ATTACH FOR EMAIL REVIEW

3 How is the title of a PDF in a shared review altered?

A SHARED COPY WILL HAVE REVIEW APPENDED TO IT.

4 What is a disadvantage of using an e-mail–based review?

PARTICIPANTS CANNOT SEE EACH OTHER COMMENTS

5 In which type of review is the PDF document stored in one location (on a server), and reviewer comments stored in another location?

BROWSER-BASED REVIEW

6 How can you collaborate with others in real time?

CREATING AN ACROBAT CONNECT MTG.

Topic B: Reviewer tools

This topic covers the following ACE exam objectives for Acrobat 8.0 Professional.

#	Objective
6.2	Conduct and manage reviews by using the Review Tracker.
6.5	Add comments to a PDF document.

The Review Tracker

Explanation

If you initiated or are participating in an automated review (such as a shared, e-mail based, or browser-based review), you can manage the review using the Review Tracker, shown in Exhibit 7-6. To open the Review Tracker, click the Review & Comment button and choose Review Tracker. You can also choose Comments, Review Tracker. The left pane shows the reviews in progress, including reviews you initiated or reviews you are participating in. When you select a review, the review details appear in the right pane, which includes the document being reviewed, the list of participants, and notification of any new comments that have been published. You can also open a review document, or you can e-mail review participants by clicking the links in the right pane.

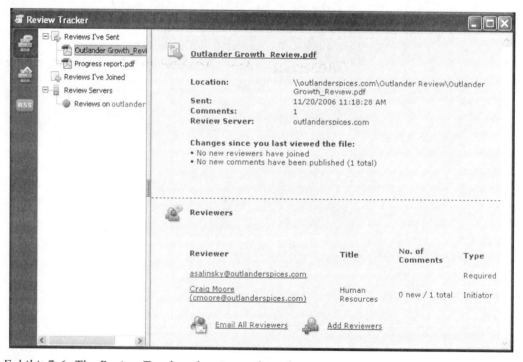

Exhibit 7-6: The Review Tracker showing a shared review in progress

Reviewing documents

If you're a participant in a review, you might want to first view any attachments or comments provided by the initiator, and then add your own comments and markups. To add comments, you need to work with the Comments & Markup toolbar, shown in Exhibit 7-7.

When a participant opens a PDF file that's part of an automated review (such as a shared review), the Comments & Markup toolbar is automatically visible. Also, in a shared review, a document message bar is visible with brief instructions and buttons for viewing and publishing new comments. If the review is non-automated, participants can open the toolbar by using several techniques:

- Click Review & Comment, and choose Show Comment & Markup toolbar.
- Choose Comments, Show Comment & Markup toolbar.
- Choose View, Toolbars, Comment & Markup.
- Choose Tools, Comment & Markup, Show Comment & Markup toolbar.

Exhibit 7-7: The Comment & Markup toolbar

Sticky notes

One way to provide feedback during a review process is to insert sticky notes. You can add a note to any part of a PDF document page. The note appears as an icon on the page. When you point to the note icon, its content appears as a tooltip. You can also click a note to open it in a pop-up window, as shown in Exhibit 7-8.

Exhibit 7-8: A sticky note with its associated pop-up window

To insert a note:

1   If necessary, open the Comment & Markup toolbar by clicking Review & Comment and then choosing Show Comment & Markup toolbar.

2   On the Comment & Markup toolbar, select the Sticky Note tool.

3   Click the page where you want to add the note. A note icon appears where you clicked, and a pop-up window appears.

4   Type to add the note text in the pop-up window.

5   If necessary, drag the note icon to move it.

6   If necessary, drag the pop-up window by its title bar to move the pop-up window.

Note properties

You can customize note properties such as note color and opacity. In the note's pop-up window, choose Options, Properties and activate the Appearance tab. Specify the desired settings, and click OK.

Do it!

B-1:   Adding notes

Here's how	Here's why
1 Open Newsletter.pdf	(From the current unit folder.) The document opens along with the Attachments panel.
Save the file as **My Newsletter**	In the current unit folder.
2 Double-click **Review checklist**	(In the Attachments panel.) The Launch attachment dialog box appears.
Select **Open this file**	If necessary.
Click **OK**	To open the attached file in Microsoft Word.
3 Close the attached file and Word	
Close the Attachments panel	
4 Click the Review & Comment button, and choose **Show Comment & Markup toolbar**	(If necessary.) To open the Comment & Markup toolbar.
5 Click [💬 Sticky Note]	(The Sticky Note tool.) You'll add a note next to the picture of the company president.
Click the white area to the left of the photo	To add a note next to the photo.
Enter **Find a higher quality photo**	In the pop-up window.

6 Point to the pop-up window title bar, as shown

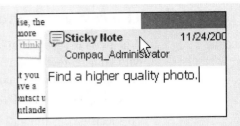

Drag the window to the right of the image

Close the pop-up window   Click the pop-up window's Close button.

7 Point to the sticky note icon

A tooltip appears, displaying the note's author name and the comment text. You'll change the note color.

8 Click the note icon   To open the pop-up window again.

9 In the pop-up window, choose **Options**, **Properties...**   To open the Sticky Note Properties dialog box.

10 Activate the Appearance tab   If necessary.

11 Click the Color swatch, and select a dark blue color   To apply the color to the note icon and its pop-up window.

Click **OK**

12 Close the note's pop-up window

The review author name

Explanation

When you review a PDF document, you should make sure that your name is associated with your review comments. By default, Acrobat uses your computer's login name as the author name for all comments. However, you can specify a different author name for individual review comments, or for all new review comments you create.

To specify a custom author name for document review comments:

1 Choose Edit, Preferences to open the Preferences dialog box.

2 Under Categories, select Commenting to view commenting preferences.

3 Under Making Comments, clear Always use Log-in Name for Author name.

4 Click OK.

5 Add a sticky note to the document. The note uses the computer login name as the author name.

6 In the sticky note pop-up window, choose Properties from the Options menu. You can also right-click the sticky note icon, and select Properties.

7 Activate the General tab.

8 In the Author box, enter the name you want to use, and click Close. This one note will use the author name you specified, but any new notes will continue to use your computer login name.

9 In the sticky note pop-up window, choose Make Current Properties Default. You can also right-click the sticky note icon and select Make Current Properties Default. Now, all new notes and comments you add will use the new name as the author name.

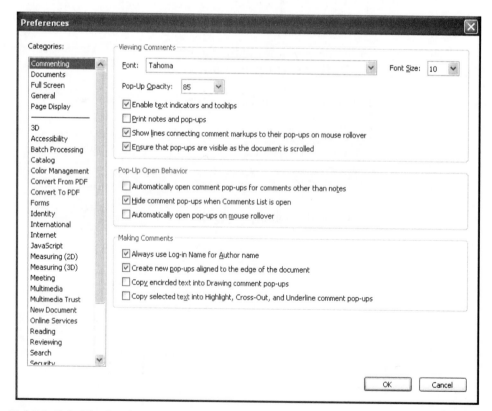

Exhibit 7-9: The Preferences dialog box

Do it!

B-2: Specifying the review author name

Here's how	Here's why
1 Choose **Edit**, **Preferences...**	To open the Preferences dialog box.
Under Categories, select **Commenting**	If necessary.
Under Making Comments, clear **Always use Log-in Name for Author name**	To allow you to specify an Author name for review notes and comments other than the computer's login name.
Click **OK**	
2 Add a sticky note anywhere on the page	Select the Sticky Note tool in the Comment & Markup toolbar, then click anywhere on the page.
3 Observe the sticky note pop-up window's title bar	The title bar shows your computer's login name.
4 In the pop-up window, choose **Options**, **Properties...**	To open the Sticky Note Properties dialog box.
Activate the General tab	To display the general note properties.
In the Author box, enter your name	
Click **OK**	To close the dialog box.
5 Observe the author name in the pop-up window	Your name appears at the top of the pop-up window. However, any new review markups you add will still use the computer login name. You'll set this note's specified author as the default for all new notes.
6 In the pop-up window, choose **Options**, **Make Current Properties Default**	All new comments and markups will use your name.
7 Click the sticky note icon to select it, and press (*DELETE*)	To remove the note you added.

Drawing markups

Explanation

In addition to adding standalone sticky notes, you can add graphic markups to draw attention to portions of the PDF document for which you want to provide feedback. You can add drawing markups in the shape of rectangles, ovals, squares, lines, and more. The Cloud tool and Dimensioning tool are particularly useful with technical drawings and blueprints. You can add a pop-up note to any drawing markup. You can select the drawing markup tools from the following locations:

- The Comment & Markup toolbar, shown in Exhibit 7-10.
- The Comments, Comment & Markup Tools submenu.
- The Tools, Comment & Markup submenu.

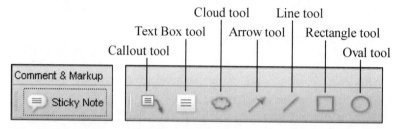

Exhibit 7-10: Markup tools in the Comment & Markup toolbar

To add a drawing markup:

1 In the Comment & Markup toolbar, select a drawing markup tool.
2 Drag on a page to add the drawing markup.
3 Click the drawing markup's edge to select it so that corner handles appear around the object; then drag the corner handles to resize the object as necessary.
4 Double-click the drawing markup's border to open its pop-up window to add a comment.
5 Click the pop-up window's Close button to close it. When you point to the edge of the drawing markup, the comment appears as a tooltip.

Do it!

B-3: Adding drawing markups

Here's how	Here's why
1 Go to page 3	You'll add an oval around part of a graphic.
2 In the Comment & Markup toolbar, click	The Oval tool.
3 Drag to draw an oval around the green area	You'll resize the oval as necessary.
4 Click the edge of the oval, as shown	To select it. Handles appear at the corners of a bounding box around the oval.
5 Point to a corner handle and drag	To resize the oval as necessary. Now you'll add a comment to the oval.
6 Double-click the oval's edge	To open the oval's pop-up window. (Notice that the pop-up window shows the author name you entered in the previous activity.)
7 Enter **Add labels for the new locations**	
Close the pop-up window	A small note icon appears next to the oval to indicate that a comment exists for it.
8 Save the document	

Text markup tools

Explanation

When you review a PDF document containing text, you can add text edit markups and text highlighting to indicate your proposed changes. These markups won't change the original document text.

To add text markups to a PDF document text by using the Text Edits tool:

1 In the Comment & Markup toolbar, select the Text Edits tool.

2 Add, delete, or modify the text:

- Point where you want to add text, click to place an insertion point, and type to add the text. A carat appears where you clicked, and the text you typed appears in a pop-up window.

- Select the text you want to remove and press Backspace or Delete. A crossout appears on the text you want to remove. You can double-click the crossout to add a comment.

- Select the text you want to change, and type to add the new text. The original word is crossed out, and the new text is added to a pop-up window.

To highlight, underline, or cross out PDF document text:

1 In the Comment & Markup toolbar, select the Text Edits tool.

2 Drag across the text you want to highlight, underline, or cross out.

3 Click the Text Edits button to expand the tool list, as shown in Exhibit 7-11. From the list, select a command.

4 Double-click the marked up text to add an associated comment.

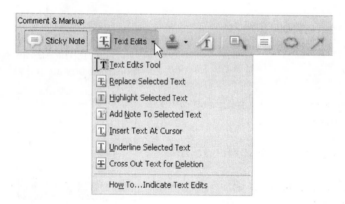

Exhibit 7-11: The Text Edits tool submenu

Do it!

B-4: Adding text markups

Here's how	Here's why
1 Verify that page 3 is visible	You'll add editing markups to some of the text on this page.
2 Choose **View**, **Zoom**, **Actual Size**	To increase the magnification so you can read the text more easily.
3 In the Comment & Markup toolbar, click [Text Edits ▾]	The Indicating Text Edits dialog box appears.
Check **Don't show again**	To keep this dialog box from appearing in the future.
Click **OK**	
4 Under the Four New Locations heading, select **very**	You'll add a markup indicating that this word should be deleted.
Press (← BACKSPACE)	

Four New Lo

After a ~~very~~ successful
retail stores, Outlander

The word appears with a red strike through it.

Here's how	Here's why
5 Go to page 4	
Scroll to view the Cooking with Chile Peppers story	You'll change the beginning of the first sentence.
6 Select the words **Ever wonder**	At the beginning of the story.
Type **Have you ever wondered**	To cross out the selected words and add the new text into the associated pop-up window.
Close the pop-up window	

Cooking with

~~Ever wonder~~ just how ho
are? Or what foods are m
with them? In 1912, a ch

A carat appears after the crossed-out text, indicating that new text exists for that location in the paragraph.

Here's how	Here's why
Point to the crossed-out text	A tooltip appears displaying the replacement text.

7	In the Comment & Markup toolbar, click ![icon]	(The Highlight Text tool.) You'll highlight some text and add a comment.
	Select the word **Chile**	(In the story heading.) To highlight the word.
8	Double-click the highlighted word	To display its pop-up window.
	Enter **Should we use the alternate spelling**, chili?	
	Close the pop-up window	
9	Save the document	

Stamps

Explanation

You can add stamps to a PDF document to indicate important information, such as the document's status. For example, when you finish reviewing a document, you can add a stamp to the first page that displays the word, "Reviewed." That way, when you send the document to others, they'll see right away that you've reviewed it. You can also add a dynamic stamp that includes your name along with the date and time, as shown in Exhibit 7-12.

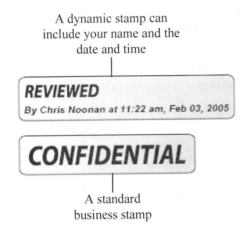

A dynamic stamp can include your name and the date and time

REVIEWED
By Chris Noonan at 11:22 am, Feb 03, 2005

CONFIDENTIAL

A standard
business stamp

Exhibit 7-12: A dynamic stamp and a standard business stamp

You can use one of Acrobat's predefined stamps, or you can create your own custom stamp. To add a predefined stamp:

1   In the Comment & Markup toolbar, click the small black triangle to the right of the Stamp tool to expand the tool list.

2   Select a stamp from one of the submenus.

3   Point to the document where you want to add the stamp, and click to add the stamp or drag to set the stamp's size.

4   Double-click the stamp to open a pop-up window, and type a comment. Click the pop-up window's Close button when you're finished.

Do it!   **B-5:   Adding a stamp**

Here's how	Here's why
1 View the top of page 1	
2 In the Comment & Markup toolbar, click	(The Stamp tool.) The Identity Setup dialog box appears.
3 In the Name box, enter your name	
In the Organization Name box, enter **Outlander Spices**	
Click **Complete**	Now you'll choose the stamp you want to add to the document.
4 Click Stamp Tool	To display the tool list.
Choose **Dynamic**, **Reviewed**	To select the Reviewed stamp.
5 Click in the top left corner of the first page	
	(You might have to move the Comment & Markup toolbar.) To add the stamp at this location, as shown.
6 Save the document	

Topic C: Manipulate comments and markups

Explanation

After you finish adding comments to a PDF file, you need to either publish the comments, or e-mail them back to the review initiator. If you're participating in an automated review, you can either publish your comments or automatically e-mail them. If you're participating in a non-automated review, you'll need to manually e-mail your copy of the PDF file back to the initiator, or you can export your comments to a Form Data Format (FDF) file and send that. Keep in mind that automated reviews require that all participants use Acrobat 6.0 or later. If you aren't sure what version of Acrobat everyone is using, you might opt to initiate a non-automated review.

Automated reviews

In automated reviews, the type of review depends on the method you use to post your comments. In a shared review, a document message bar is visible, as shown in Exhibit 7-13. To publish your comments, click Publish Comments. You can also use the message bar to check for comments posted by other participants, or open the Review Tracker.

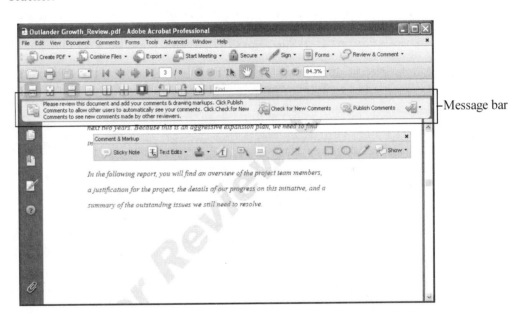

Exhibit 7-13: A shared review document showing the message bar

In an e-mail-based review, the document message bar is visible, and the Send Comments button is automatically added to the Comment & Markup toolbar, as shown in Exhibit 7-14. Clicking Send Comments instructs Acrobat to automatically e-mail the PDF back to the review initiator.

Exhibit 7-14: The Send Comments button in the Comment & Markup toolbar

Non-automated reviews

In a non-automated review, you'll need to either e-mail the entire PDF file back to the review initiator, or export your comments to an FDF file and send that. The exported FDF file contains only the review comments and markups, so it's typically much smaller than the PDF document. When the review initiator receives comments in FDF files from you and other reviewers, the review initiator can import all those comments into a single PDF document.

To export review comments and markups to an FDF file:

1 In the Navigation pane, click the Comments icon to activate the Comments panel, shown in Exhibit 7-15. (You can also choose Comments, Comment View, Show Comments List.) The comments are grouped by page.

2 If you want to export only some of the comments, select the ones you want to export.

- Shift+click comments to select a range.

- Ctrl+click to select comments one at a time.

- Choose Edit, Select All to select all comments, and then Ctrl-click to deselect the ones you don't want.

3 Export the comments.

- If you want to export only the selected comments, choose Options, Export Selected Comments.

- If you want to export all comments, choose Options, Export Comments to Data File.

4 E-mail or otherwise provide the FDF file containing your comments to the review initiator.

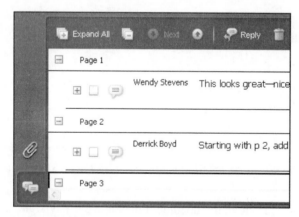

Exhibit 7-15: Comments in the Comments List

Do it!

C-1: Exporting comments and markups

Here's how	Here's why
1 Click	(The Comments icon is in the Navigation pane.) To activate the Comments panel. The comments are ordered by page. You'll export all comments except the "Reviewed" stamp.
2 Observe the list of comments	An icon next to each comment identifies the comment type. You'll export these comments as an FDF file.
3 Click any comment in the list	To select it.
Press `CTRL` + `A`	To select all the comments. You'll deselect the stamp comment.
4 Hold down `CTRL` and click the stamp comment	

To deselect it.

5 In the commands at the top of the Comments List, click **Options**	To display the Options menu.
Choose **Export Selected Comments...**	To open the Export Comments dialog box. You'll name the file using your initials followed by the word "Reviewed."
In the File Name box, enter your initials followed by "Comments"	To name the comments file.
Navigate to the current unit folder and click **Save**	
6 Save and close the document	

Compile comments

When a document review is complete, the review initiator will compile the review comments from all the reviewers. The procedure for compiling the review comments differs based on the type of review workflow. Part of the procedure is automated when you're using a shared, e-mail–based, or browser-based review. But whichever review workflow you use, you'll need to organize and go through the comments after they're compiled.

Importing comments

If you're using a non-automated review workflow, you'll need to use the Import Comments command to import the FDF files from the reviewers.

To import reviewer comments from FDF files:

1 Open the PDF document in which you want to compile the reviewer comments.

2 Choose Comments, Import Comments to open the Import Comments dialog box.

3 Navigate to and select the FDF file containing the comments you want to import, and click Select. A dialog box might appear, indicating that the comments were created in a different version of the document. Click OK, if necessary. The comments you import appear in the document, and are listed in the Comments List by page number.

Do it!

C-2: Importing comments from multiple reviewers

Here's how	Here's why
1 Open My Initiate review.pdf	If you added an attachment earlier, the Attachments panel might be visible.
Close the Attachments panel	(If necessary.) You'll import existing comments.
2 Choose **Comments, Import Comments...**	To open the Import Comments dialog box.
Select **DboydReview.fdf**	In the current unit folder.
Hold down ⌈CTRL⌉ and select **WstevensReview.fdf**	To select both files.
Click **Select**	To import the comments. A dialog box appears, indicating that the comments were created in a different version of the document.
3 Click **Yes**	(If necessary.) To import the first comment file.
Click **Yes** again	
	(If necessary.) To import the second comment file. The comments from both reviewers appear in the Comments List.
4 Save the file	

Navigating reviewer comments

Explanation

After you compile comments from all reviewers into a single PDF document, you can use the Comments List options to organize and examine the comments. Some of the options on the Comments List are unavailable if no comments are selected. When you select a comment in the Comments List, you navigate to that comment within the PDF document, and the comment is automatically highlighted on the page. The following table describes the tools you can use to navigate reviewer comments.

Tool	Description
Expand All	Click to expand all items in the Comments list.
	Click to collapse all items.
Next	Click to select the next comment.
	Click to select the previous comment.
Reply	Click to add a reply to the selected comment. Your comment is added as a reply within the comment's pop-up window.
	Click to delete the selected comment.
Set Status ▾	From this list, select a status for the selected comment. You can specify a status for each comment to help you or others know how to handle each comment. You can set a comment's status as Accepted, Rejected, Cancelled, or Completed, and can hide or show comments based on their status.
Checkmark	Click to add a check mark in the check box next to the selected comment, or click the check box directly. You can add check marks for any purpose, such as to help you remember which comments you've already looked at. Check marks won't appear when others view the PDF file.
Show ▾	From this list, select a category of comments you want to show, hiding all others. You can show comments based on type, reviewer, status, or checked state.
Sort By ▾	From this list, specify how you want to order the comments. You can order the comments by type, page, author, date, color, or checkmark status.
	Click to search for specific comment text.

Tool	Description
Print Comments ▾	From this list you can either print a summary of the review comments, or you can create a PDF document summarizing the review comments.
Options ▾ ✖	From this list, you can import comments, export comments, create a summary of the review comments, or open the Tracker. The Tracker lists all the PDF documents that you've sent or received for review via e-mail-based or browser-based review.

Do it!

C-3: Navigating comments from multiple reviewers

Here's how	Here's why
1 In the Comments List, click [A Z ↕ Sort By ▾]	To display the Sort By list.
Choose **Author**	A dialog box might appear, describing the Show and Sort menus and the Search button.
Click **OK**	(If necessary.) The review comments are sorted by author.
2 Next to Derrick Boyd's name, click [+]	To show the comments from Derrick Boyd.
3 Select Derrick Boyd's first comment	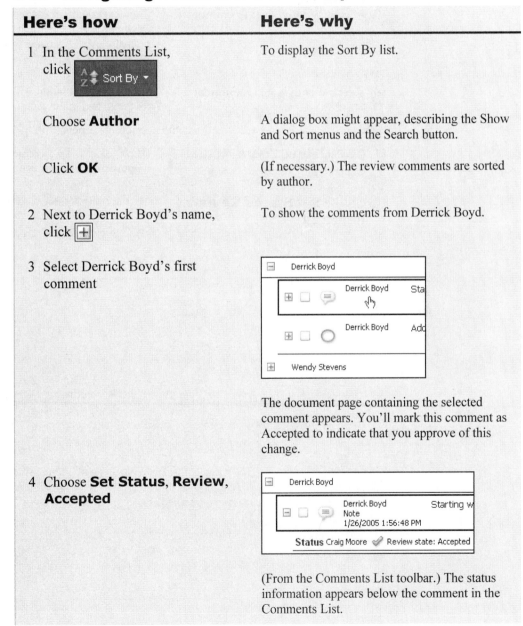
	The document page containing the selected comment appears. You'll mark this comment as Accepted to indicate that you approve of this change.
4 Choose **Set Status**, **Review**, **Accepted**	
	(From the Comments List toolbar.) The status information appears below the comment in the Comments List.

5	Click ⬇ Next	To navigate to the next comment.
6	Accept the comment	Choose Set Status, Review, Accepted.
7	Select the first comment from Wendy Stevens	Expand Wendy's comments, then click her first comment to select it. This comment is just a note to you, and doesn't require any change to the document.
8	Choose **Set Status**, **Review**, **Completed**	To indicate that this comment doesn't require any further action.
9	Accept Wendy's next comment	The next comment is a note that Thomas Boorman will be handing the project over to a colleague, and his name will have to be changed when the replacement is determined.
10	Select Wendy's next comment	(Click the Next button.) The next comment is a text edit, and might be too small to see on the document page.
11	Choose **View**, **Zoom**, **Actual Size**	(If necessary.) To increase the document magnification so you can read the text.
12	Choose **Set Status**, **Review**, **Rejected**	To mark this comment as rejected.

Comment summaries

Explanation   ✳   After going through all the review comments, you'll either make the changes to the document in the original program used to create it, or you'll pass the comments on to someone else to make the changes. To ensure that only the changes you approve of will be made to the original document, you can create a document that lists only the review comments that you've accepted.

To create a comment summary containing only the accepted comments:

1 In the Comments List, choose Show, Show By Status, Review, Accepted. Only the comments marked as Accepted are now visible in the Comments List.

2 Choose Options, Summarize Comments to open the Summarize Options dialog box, shown in Exhibit 7-16.

3 Under Choose a Layout, select the type of layout you want to create.

4 Next to Include, select Only the comments currently showing.

5 Click Create PDF Comment Summary to create and display the comments summary file.

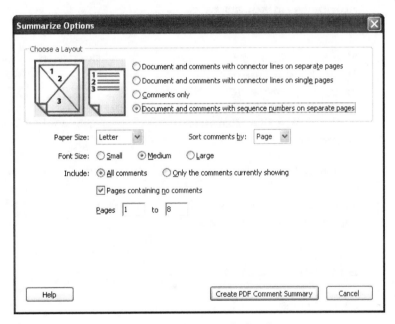

Exhibit 7-16: The Summarize Options dialog box

Do it!

C-4: Creating a comment summary PDF file

Here's how	Here's why
1 Click [Show ▾]	To display the Show menu.
Choose **Show By Status**, **Review**, **Accepted**	(From the Show menu.) To show only comments you marked as Accepted.
Click **OK**	(If necessary.) Comments you marked as Rejected or Completed are hidden.
2 Choose **Options**, **Summarize Comments...**	To open the Summarize Options dialog box.
3 Select **Document and comments with sequence numbers on separate pages**	If necessary.
Next to Include, select **Only the comments currently showing**	To include only the Accepted comments, which are the only ones currently showing.
Click **Create PDF Comment Summary**	To create the new PDF document summarizing the accepted comments.
4 Switch to the new document	If necessary.
View each page and its associated page of comment summaries	You'll save the comment summary PDF file.
5 Save the file as **Summary of comments**	In the current unit folder.
6 Save and close all files	

Unit summary: Document review techniques

Topic A   In this topic, you learned about **PDF document review techniques**. You added a **file attachment**, and created and customized a **watermark** to indicate the document's review status. You also learned how to initiate **shared**, **e-mail–based**, and **browser-based** automated reviews.

Topic B   In this topic, you opened a PDF document attachment. You also specified the author name for **review comments**, and you learned how to add **notes**, **markups**, and **stamps**. Finally, you exported your review comments and markups to an **FDF file**.

Topic C   In this topic, you **imported FDF files** containing review comments. You also sorted and viewed review comments from multiple reviewers. Then you specified the **review status** for how each comment should be handled, and you created a **comment summary file** containing selected comments.

Independent practice activity

In this activity, you'll add an attachment and a watermark to a PDF document. You'll also add reviewer markups to a PDF document, and you'll export your comments to an FDF file. Finally, you'll import and view comments from other reviewers.

1 Open Initiate review practice.pdf from the current unit folder.

2 Save the file as **My Initiate review practice** in the current unit folder.

3 Add the Attachment practice.rtf file as an attachment.

4 Add a text watermark displaying the word **Confidential** using formatting settings of your choice.

5 Save and close the document.

6 Open Review practice.pdf and save it as **My Review practice**.

7 Under the "All spiced up" heading, before the word "foods" in the second line, add a text markup to insert the word **gourmet**.

8 Under the "Expansion project" heading, add a text markup indicating that the word "very" near the end of the paragraph should be deleted.

9 Add an oval around the project team members, and add an associated note that reads **Several people are missing from this list**.

10 Export all your comments to an FDF file named **My Review practice**.

11 Save and close all files.

12 Open My Initiate review practice.pdf.

13 Import the review comments from the NCalvertReview practice.fdf file.

14 View each comment and mark each one as **Accepted**.

15 Create a comment summary file that includes all the reviewer comments, and use the Document and comments with sequence numbers on separate pages layout.

16 Save the file in the current unit folder as **My Review summary practice**.

17 Save and close all files.

18 Close Acrobat.

Review questions

1   How can you attach a document to a PDF file?

   A   Choose Tools, Advanced Editing, Link Tool.

   B   Choose Document, Attach a File.

   C   Choose File, Create PDF, From Multiple Files.

   D   Drag the document to the Pages tab.

2   How can you add a graphic or text item that appears on every page of a PDF file?

   A   Choose Document, Attach a File.

   B   Select all the thumbnails in the Pages tab; then choose Document, Insert Pages.

   C   Choose Document, Add Watermark & Background.

   D   Choose Document, Add Headers & Footers.

3   How can you start a document review process over the Web?

   A   Choose File, Send For Review, Upload For Browser-Based Review.

   B   Choose File, Send For Review, Send by Email for Review.

   C   Choose Comments, Enable for Commenting in Adobe Reader.

   D   Choose Comments, Export Comments, To Word.

4   You want to begin a document review in which all participants can see the comments made by other reviewers. Which type of review should you use?

   A   An E-mail–based review

   B   A Browser-based review

   C   A non-automated review

   D   A paper-based review

5   You want to automate a document review, but you don't have any Web server space available to use. Which type of review can you use?

   A   An E-mail–based review

   B   A Browser-based review

   C   A non-automated review

   D   A paper-based review

6   How can you start an Acrobat Connect meeting? (Choose all that apply.)

   A   Choose File, Start Meeting.

   B   In the Tasks toolbar, click the Start Meeting button.

   C   Right-click anywhere on the document and choose Start Meeting.

   D   Triple-click anywhere on the document.

7 How can you open the Review Tracker? (Choose all that apply.)

A Right-click anywhere on the document and choose Review Tracker.

B In the Tasks toolbar, click the Review & Comment button.

C Triple-click anywhere on the document.

D Choose Comments, Review Tracker.

8 You've been asked to review a PDF file. Which tools can you use to add comments to the file? (Choose all that apply.)

A The Select tool

B The Text TouchUp tool

C The Sticky Note tool

D The Stamp tool

Appendix A

ACE exam objectives map

This appendix provides the following information:

A ACE exam objectives for Acrobat 8.0 Professional with references to corresponding coverage in ILT Series courseware.

Topic A: ACE exam objectives

Explanation

The following table lists the Adobe Certified Expert (ACE) exam objectives for Acrobat 8.0 Professional and indicates where each objective is covered in conceptual explanations, hands-on activities, or both.

#	Objective	Course level	Conceptual information	Supporting activities
1.1	Describe the benefits and functionality provided by Acrobat Connect.	Basic	Unit 7, Topic A	A-3
1.2	Describe the options available for customizing toolbars.	Basic	Unit 1, Topic A	A-2
1.3	Describe the functionality provided to users of Adobe Reader by using the Enable Usage Rights command.	Advanced	Unit 6, Topic A	A-4
1.4	Convert an Adobe PDF document to another format by using the File > Export command.	Advanced	Unit 6, Topic A	A-3
1.5	Manage and modify PDF documents by using the Advanced > Document Processing commands.	Advanced	Unit 6, Topic A	A-2
2.1	Explain how to access and use navigation features in a PDF document.	Basic	Unit 1, Topic A Unit 1, Topic B	A-3 B-1, B-2
2.2	Use Find/Search to locate specific information in PDF documents.	Basic	Unit 1, Topic C	C-1, C-2
2.3	Given a viewing tool, explain the purpose of or how to use that tool. (Tools include: Zoom, Scrolling, Go To, Hand)	Basic	Unit 1, Topic A	
3.1	List and describe the methods available for creating PDF documents. (Methods include: From a Scanner, from a File)	Basic Advanced	Unit 2, Topic C Unit 1, Topic A	A-2
3.2	Create a PDF document by using Adobe PDF Printer.	Basic Advanced	Unit 2, Topic A Unit 1, Topic C	A-1 C-4
3.3	Create a PDF document by using Adobe PDFMaker.	Basic	Unit 2, Topic B	B-1
3.4	Create a PDF document by using Acrobat Distiller.	Advanced	Unit 1, Topic B Unit 1, Topic C	B-1 C-1, C-2, C-3
4.1	List and describe the options available for combining files. (Options include: merging files into a single PDF document, assembling files into a PDF Package, creating PDF packages in Microsoft Outlook and Lotus Notes, identifying differences between the Windows and Mac platforms)	Basic	Unit 2, Topic C	

#	Objective	Course level	Conceptual information	Supporting activities
4.2	Manage how files are combined and optimized by using the Combine Files dialog box.	Basic	Unit 2, Topic C	C-1
4.3	Incorporate headers, footers, watermarks and backgrounds to a PDF document.	Basic	Unit 3, Topic B Unit 7, Topic A	B-3 A-2
4.4	Attach files to a PDF document.	Basic	Unit 7, Topic A	A-1
5.1	Explain how to modify PDF documents by selecting options from the Document menu.	Basic	Unit 3, Topic A Unit 3, Topic B	
5.2	Given a tool on the Advanced Editing toolbar, explain how to use that tool. (Tools include: Link, Crop, TouchUp Text, TouchUp Object, Movie, Sound)	Basic	Unit 3, Topic B	B-1, B-2
5.3	Create and modify bookmarks.	Basic	Unit 4, Topic A	A-1-A-6
5.4	Rearrange and number pages by using the Pages panel.	Basic	Unit 3, Topic A Unit 3, Topic B	A-1 B-4
5.5	Given a scenario, optimize the size of a PDF document by using the PDF Optimizer.	Basic	Unit 3, Topic D	D-1
6.1	Given a scenario, describe the methods available for conducting a review, and when you would use that method.	Basic	Unit 7, Topic A	
6.2	Conduct and manage reviews by using the Review Tracker.	Basic	Unit 7, Topic B	
6.3	Explain how to set up an E-mail review of an Adobe PDF document.	Basic	Unit 7, Topic A	A-3
6.4	Explain how to set up shared review of an Adobe PDF document.	Basic	Unit 7, Topic A	A-3
6.5	Add comments to a PDF document.	Basic	Unit 7, Topic B	B-1, B-3, B-4, B-5
7.1	List and describe methods that can be used to secure a PDF document by using passwords	Basic	Unit 6, Topic A	A-1, A-2, A-3
7.2	List and describe the methods available for creating and acquiring digital signatures and certificates	Basic	Unit 6, Topic B	B-1, B-2
7.3	Certify a document by applying a digital signature.	Basic	Unit 6, Topic B	B-3, B-4, B-5
7.4	Secure documents by creating a security envelope.	Basic	Unit 6, Topic C	C-2

#	Objective	Course level	Conceptual information	Supporting activities
7.5	Describe the functionality provided by Adobe LiveCycle Policy Server for encrypting PDF documents.	Basic	Unit 6, Topic D	D-1
7.6	Examine documents for and remove hidden data by using the Redaction commands.	Advanced	Unit 6, Topic A	A-1
8.1	Given a specific output requirement, choose the appropriate Adobe PDF Setting.	Advanced	Unit 1, Topic B	B-1
8.2	Given a specific output requirement, create a customized Adobe PDF Setting.	Advanced	Unit 1, Topic C Unit 2, Topic B	C-1 through C-4 B-2
9.1	Compare and contrast the functionality provided for creating forms by using Adobe LiveCycle Designer versus using the Acrobat forms tools.	Advanced	Unit 5, Topic A Unit 5, Topic B Unit 5, Topic C Unit 5, Topic D	A-1, A-2 B-1 through B-5 C-1 through C-7 D-1, D-2, D-3
9.2	Explain the functionality provided by the Form Field Recognition features.	Advanced	Unit 5, Topic B	B-1
9.3	Compile and manage form data.	Advanced	Unit 6, Topic B	B-1, B-2
10.1	List and describe the features and options made available through the Print Production toolbar.	Advanced	Unit 2, Topic C Unit 2, Topic D Unit 3, Topic A Unit 3, Topic B Unit 3, Topic C Unit 3, Topic D Unit 3, Topic E	C-1 D-1 A-2, A-3 B-1 C-1 D-2 E-1, E-2
10.2	Given an option in the Output Preview dialog box, explain the purpose of that option.	Advanced	Unit 2, Topic C Unit 3, Topic B	C-1 B-1, B-2
10.3	Given an option in the Preflight dialog box, explain the purpose of that option. (Options include: execute a preflight profile, create a custom preflight profile, create a preflight droplet)	Advanced	Unit 4, Topic B Unit 4, Topic C Unit 4, Topic D Unit 4, Topic E	B-1, B-2 C-1 D-1 E-1

Course summary

This summary contains information to help you bring the course to a successful conclusion. Using this information, you will be able to:

A Use the summary text to reinforce what you've learned in class.

B Determine the next courses in this series (if any), as well as any other resources that might help you continue to learn about Acrobat 8.0 Professional.

Topic A: Course summary

Use the following summary text to reinforce what you've learned in class.

Unit summaries

Unit 1

In this unit, you identified the **benefits of PDF**, and you learned how to **navigate PDF documents** using **bookmarks** and **links**. Then you learned how to **search PDF documents**, and open and **organize** PDF documents by using the **Organizer** window. Finally, you learned how to access **Acrobat Help**.

Unit 2

In this unit, you learned how to use the **Adobe PDF printer** to create a PDF document from any program's Print command. You also used the **PDFMaker** to create a PDF document from other applications. Finally, you used the **Create PDF** commands in Acrobat to create PDF documents from **multiple files** and from **Web pages**.

Unit 3

In this unit, you used the **Pages panel** to **arrange pages**, **move pages** between documents, **delete pages**, and **extract pages**. You also learned how to **modify PDF document text**, add **headers and footers**, and modify **page numbering**. Then you learned how to use the Copy and Paste commands to **copy PDF content** to other programs. Finally, you learned how to use the **PDF Optimizer** to reduce PDF file size.

Unit 4

In this unit, you **created bookmarks** and modified bookmarks to change their **destinations**. You also **arranged**, **nested**, and **formatted** bookmarks. Then you created **links** using the Link tool, and **resized** and **aligned** links to the **anchor object**. Finally, you learned how to create links based on selected text.

Unit 5

In this unit, you learned how to add **tags** to a PDF document and create a new **tag structure** for a PDF document. You also learned how to check a file's **accessibility,** fix accessibility problems, and use the **Setup Accessibility Assistant** to customize accessibility preferences in the Acrobat environment. Then you learned how to customize **accessibility preferences** by using the Preferences dialog box. Finally, you learned how to use the **Read Out Loud** feature.

Unit 6

In this unit, you learned how to specify a **Document Open password** and a **Permissions password**. You also created and used **digital IDs** and validated a **digital signature**. You learned how to **encrypt** PDF files based on user **certificates** and by using **Adobe Policy Server**, and finally, you learned how to create **password** and **certificate security policies**.

Unit 7

In this unit, you learned how to add a **file attachment** and a **watermark** to a PDF document. You also learned how to initiate **automated reviews**. You added **review comments** and **markups**, and exported comments and markups to an **FDF file**. Finally, you **imported**, **managed**, and **summarized** review comments from multiple reviewers.

Topic B: Continued learning after class

It is impossible to learn to use any software effectively in a single day. To get the most out of this class, you should begin working with Adobe Acrobat 8.0 Professional to perform real tasks as soon as possible. We also offer resources for continued learning.

Next course in this series

This is the first course in this series. The next course in this series is:

- *Acrobat 8.0 Professional: Advanced, ACE Edition*

Other resources

For more information, visit www.courseilt.com.

Acrobat 8 Professional: Basic

Quick reference

Button	Shortcut keys	Function
100%	CTRL + 1	Displays document pages at actual size (100% magnification).
	CTRL + 0	Displays document pages at Fit Page view.
↔	CTRL + 2	Displays document pages at Fit Width view.
		Displays documents using Single Page layout, which shows a single document page at a time.
		Displays documents using Continuous page layout, which allows you to view more than one page at a time.
		Displays documents using Continuous - Facing page layout, which arranges document pages in pairs, as they'd appear when printed and bound.
		Displays documents using Facing page layout, which arranges document pages in pairs, as they'd appear when printed and bound. You can view only one set of facing pages at a time.
◀|	HOME	Go to the first document page.
←	←	Go to the previous document page.
→	→	Go to the next document page.
▶|	END	Go to the last document page.
●	ALT + ←	Go to the previous view.

Button	Shortcut keys	Function
	`ALT` + `→`	Go to the next view
	`CTRL` + `SHIFT` + `1`	Open the Organizer window.

Glossary

Adobe PDF printer

A tool that converts files created in any application to a PDF document. When you install Acrobat, the Adobe PDF printer is added automatically to the list of available printers.

Adobe Policy Server

A Web-based security system that you can use to control document security dynamically for your PDF documents.

Bookmarks

Text entries stored in the Bookmarks panel that you can click to navigate to specific content in the document or to perform some other action.

Collections

Groups of PDF documents that you've associated with a particular folder in the Organizer. Collections contain aliases of PDF documents, so you can associate any PDF document with any collection without changing the location of the document on your computer.

Digital ID

A file that uniquely identifies you as a user, which you can use to sign documents and generate a certificate file.

Digital signature

An electronic stamp that you can attach to a PDF file to uniquely identify yourself.

Distiller

An application installed with Acrobat that converts PostScript files to PDF. For example, when you use the Adobe PDF printer to convert a file to PostScript format, the PostScript file is sent automatically to Distiller, which converts the PostScript file to PDF.

Footer

Information that repeats at the bottom of each page in a document.

Header

Information that repeats at the top of each page in a document.

Link

PDF document content you can click to navigate to other content or perform an action. Links are typically applied to text or graphics.

Optical character recognition (OCR)

A process that identifies the text characters in a scanned document to make the document text searchable. When you apply OCR to a scanned document, the searchable text is added in an invisible background layer below the original scanned content.

Optimize

To achieve the best balance between small file size and document properties, based on the document's intended use.

PDFMaker

A component added to several Microsoft Office and other programs when you install Acrobat. You can use PDFMaker from within any of these programs to convert documents to PDF without using the Print command.

Portable Document Format (PDF)

A format that preserves the fonts, layout, colors, and graphics of any document, regardless of the program or platform used to create the original document. You can use Adobe Acrobat to convert documents to PDF and to view and modify PDF documents.

Screen magnifier

An assistive technology that displays content at an increased magnification to help people with impaired vision.

Screen reader

Software that identifies the content displayed onscreen and reads it aloud or converts it to Braille characters on a Braille device.

Security policies

Security settings you can specify and save so that you can quickly apply them to other files.

Stamp

An element you can add to a PDF document page to communicate important information, such as the document's status.

Watermarks and backgrounds

Text or images that you can add to a PDF file to repeat on each page, often to indicate the document's status.

Index